Nǐ Hǎo

Chinese Language Course
Introductory Level

(Traditional character edition)

正體字版

by

Shumang Fredlein ● Paul Fredlein

Cheng & Tsui Company, Boston

Nǐ Hǎo 1 – Chinese Language Course
Introductory Level
(Traditional character edition)

The traditional character edition of Ni Hao 1 was published by ChinaSoft in 1995 and a North American edition was published by Cheng & Tsui in 2001.

This renewed North American edition was published in 2002 by
Cheng & Tsui Company
25 West Street
Boston, MA 02111-1213 USA
Fax (617) 426-3669
www.cheng-tsui.com
"Bringing Asia to the World"™
by arrangement with ChinaSoft Pty Ltd, Australia
Web: http://www.chinasoft.com.au

Written by Shumang Fredlein (林淑滿) & Paul Fredlein
Illustrated by Xiaolin Xue (薛曉林), Zhengdong Su (蘇正東), Bo Wu (吳波), Xudong Zhu (朱旭東)
Edited by Sitong Jan (詹絲桐), Xiaolin Xue (薛曉林)
Typeset by ChinaSoft on Apple Macintosh

Companion workbook, audio tapes and CD-ROMs are also available.

ISBN 978-0-88727-363-6
17 16 15 14 13 12 11 10 09
10 9 8 7 6
Printed in the United States of America

Preface

It has been ten years since the Ni Hao series was first published. I am glad that it has been receiving such strong support from teachers and students throughout the world. Many have shown their approval and provided us with advice and suggestions. It is our goal to keep improving the series. This new edition is our attempt to achieve this goal.

In Ni Hao 1, there are more reading materials linking and consolidating the language introduced in different lessons. These new items are spiced with humor to make learning more interesting. Another print color is also added to make the book more appealing.

The revision work has been made easier with new members joining the editing team. Thanks to Sitong and Xiaolin who contribute their professional skills and knowledge in all areas needed. Their devotion and effort has smoothed the working process. Paul's interest in programming has turned the Ni Hao series into a multimedia integrated language learning course and has made the series more complete.

I would like to thank my daughter Jemma and my son David who grew up with the books. Watching their learning process and hearing their comments on the books always sparks me with new ideas.

Many thanks are owed to Juanita Yuan who provided us with teaching material at the beginning stage. I would also like to thank Lin Song, Peter Chan, Lily Dong, Chris Kain, Jessy Tu, Lisa Allen and many other teachers, who provided their advice and suggestions that led to the new look of this edition.

Shumang

Contents

Introduction

你好 Nǐ Hǎo is a basic course for beginning students of Chinese. It introduces Chinese language and culture and aims to teach communication in both spoken and written Chinese. The objectives are to enable students to use Chinese in the classroom, playground, local community and countries where the Chinese language is spoken.

The text is richly illustrated, providing a stimulating language learning tool to motivate students. Characters are used throughout the text to enhance the students' reading and writing ability. Pinyin only acts as a guide to pronunciation. When it appears on top of the characters, no capital letter is used at the beginning of the sentence and no full stop is employed. As learning progresses, the Pinyin of the characters that students have learned is omitted. To equip students to read authentic materials, various print fonts are used: Kǎishū [楷書], used in the main text, is an ideal font for students to learn to write; Sòngtǐ [宋體], used in the sentence patterns, is a font commonly used in newspapers and general publications; while Hēitǐ [黑體] is only used for titles. Apart from print fonts, various hand-written scripts are included to provide students with the opportunity to read handwriting. With reference to the current use of simplified characters in China, the simplified form is included in the vocabulary list in the appendix.

Each unit of the text in this book includes the subsections:

Illustrated texts
Learn the sentences
New words and expressions
Write the characters
Supplementary words
Something to know

In *Illustrated texts*, each conversation is based on daily life with the language in a spiralled structure. The illustrations assist in the interpretation of the conversation and are ideally suited to role playing. Grammar explanations in *Learn the sentences* are simple and illustrated with examples to clarify usage. Students can also use this section to hold conversations with partners. In *New words and expressions*, the meaning of the separate characters in each word will assist students to understand the structure of the word. The section *Supplementary words* provides students who progress quickly with additional learning material. Characters that the students should learn to write have the stroke order clearly illustrated in *Write the characters*. It is essential to write characters in the correct stroke order. Culture related to the content of the lesson is introduced in *Something to know*, a section designed to enrich cultural understanding and generate interest in learning the language.

In addition to the six subsections, songs, rhymes, tongue twisters, cartoons, little stories and interesting features of Chinese characters also play important roles in the book. They are light and cheerful materials offering wonderful opportunities for practice and reinforcement.

The Ni Hao series is a complete learning course which comprises five levels. Each level contains a textbook, a workbook, a teacher's handbook, a set of audio cassettes (or CDs), a CD-ROM games software and a CD-ROM language lab software. The textbook – *Chinese Language Course, Introductory Level* – features the basic daily language in various topics and settings and is structured, accumulative and reinforced. The student workbook contains a variety of tasks and activities using all four communication skills. The audio cassettes include all language sections in the book and the listening comprehension sections in the workbook. The handbook provides the teacher notes, suggested activities and materials that can be reproduced for class use including worksheets and flashcards. The games software allows students to revise the use of language in different settings, to use the mouse to write characters in the correct stroke order, and to challenge their memory in phrases and characters. The language lab software moves the traditional language lab to the personal computer. It allows students to interact while listening, repeating or role-playing. Students' voice can be recorded and replayed. Both programs are ideal for either class use or students' personal use.

For students who wish to learn simplified characters, a complete series of simplified character edition is published by ChinaSoft Pty Ltd in Australia.

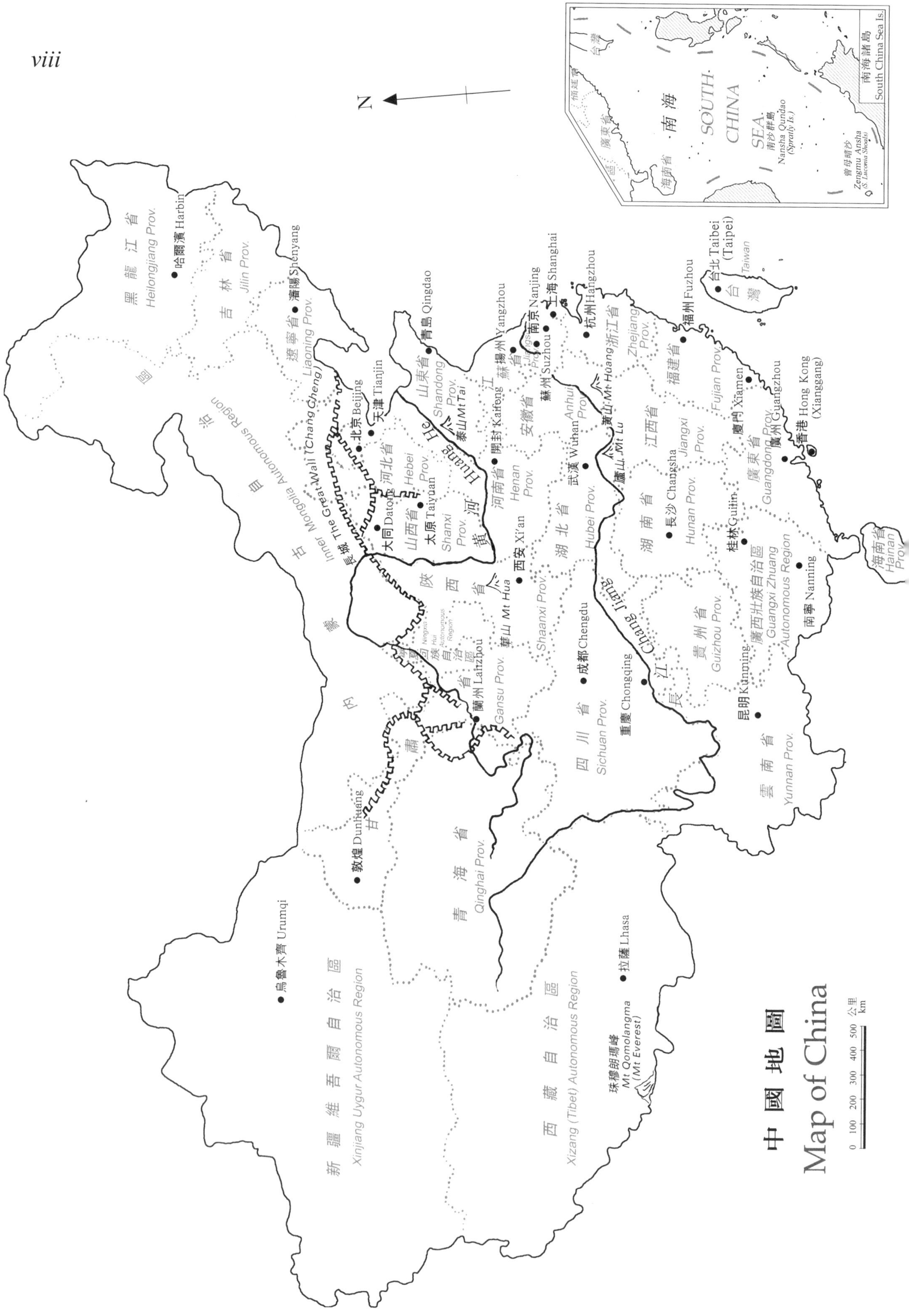

中國地圖 Map of China

N

0 100 200 300 400 500 公里 km

新疆維吾爾自治區 Xinjiang Uygur Autonomous Region
烏魯木齊 Urumqi
西藏自治區 Xizang (Tibet) Autonomous Region
拉薩 Lhasa
珠穆朗瑪峰 Mt Qomolangma (Mt Everest)
青海省 Qinghai Prov.
甘肅省 Gansu Prov.
敦煌 Dunhuang
蘭州 Lanzhou
寧夏回族自治區 Ningxia Hui Autonomous Region
內蒙古自治區 Inner Mongolia Autonomous Region
長城 The Great Wall (Chang Cheng)
黑龍江省 Heilongjiang Prov.
哈爾濱 Harbin
吉林省 Jilin Prov.
遼寧省 Liaoning Prov.
瀋陽 Shenyang
北京 Beijing
天津 Tianjin
河北省 Hebei Prov.
山西省 Shanxi Prov.
大同 Datong
太原 Taiyuan
陝西省 Shaanxi Prov.
西安 Xi'an
華山 Mt Hua
黃河 Huang He
山東省 Shandong Prov.
青島 Qingdao
泰山 Mt Tai
河南省 Henan Prov.
開封 Kaifeng
江蘇省 Jiangsu Prov.
揚州 Yangzhou
南京 Nanjing
蘇州 Suzhou
上海 Shanghai
安徽省 Anhui Prov.
黃山 Mt Huang
浙江省 Zhejiang Prov.
杭州 Hangzhou
湖北省 Hubei Prov.
武漢 Wuhan
廬山 Mt Lu
江西省 Jiangxi Prov.
福建省 Fujian Prov.
福州 Fuzhou
廈門 Xiamen
台灣 Taiwan
台北 Taibei (Taipei)
四川省 Sichuan Prov.
成都 Chengdu
重慶 Chongqing
長江 Chang Jiang
湖南省 Hunan Prov.
長沙 Changsha
貴州省 Guizhou Prov.
雲南省 Yunnan Prov.
昆明 Kunming
廣西壯族自治區 Guangxi Zhuang Autonomous Region
桂林 Guilin
南寧 Nanning
廣東省 Guangdong Prov.
廣州 Guangzhou
香港 Hong Kong (Xianggang)
海南省 Hainan Prov.

南海 SOUTH CHINA SEA
南沙群島 Nansha Qundao (Spratly Is.)
曾母暗沙 Zengmu Ansha (S. Luconia Shoals)
南海諸島 South China Sea Is.

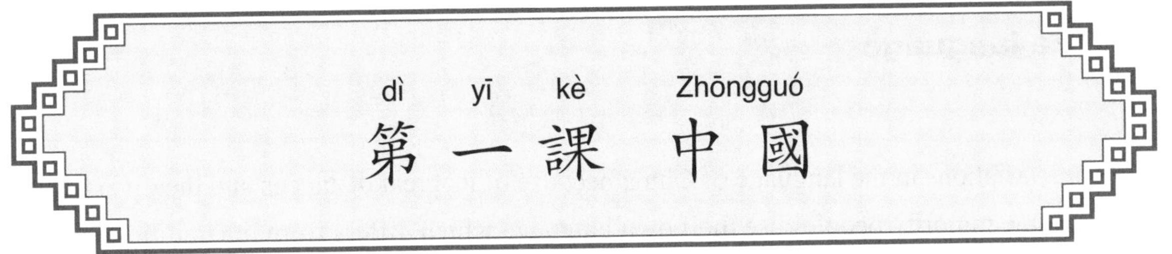

dì yī kè Zhōngguó
第一課 中國

1 The country

China is situated in the eastern part of the Asian continent and is the third largest country in the world. It covers a total area of approximately 3.7 million square miles and is a land of contrasts with deserts in the north, mountains in the south and cultivated areas in the east.

This vast land supports almost a quarter of the world's population: over one billion people of different races, traditions and cultures. Although the majority (about 94% of the population) are the Han people, there are fifty-five minority peoples, the largest among them being the Mongolians [蒙古族 Ménggǔzú], the Tibetans [藏族 Zàngzú] and the Zhuang [壯族 Zhuàngzú].

Chinese culture was the cradle of Japanese, Korean and some South East Asian cultures. The ancient Chinese considered their country to be the center of the world and called it Zhōngguó [中國], literally meaning 'the Central Kingdom'.

2 The language

There are variations in the language of China because of its great distances and the diversity of its people. Some minority peoples use their own language which differs from the traditional Chinese language. Those who use the traditional language (around 80% of the Chinese population) have developed regional differences in pronunciation, words and grammar. These variations are called *dialects*. People who speak one dialect sometimes find it difficult to understand the speech of someone who speaks another. Just as an American might have difficulty understanding a strong Scottish accent, so too people who only speak Cantonese [廣東話 Guǎngdōnghuà] may have trouble talking with people who only speak the Min dialect [福建話 Fújiànhuà]. However, people who speak different dialects can always communicate with each other in the written language, which was unified by the First Emperor [秦始皇 Qín Shǐhuáng] (221–210 BC).

Although the written Chinese language was the same, there were still problems in communication caused by the many dialects. To solve these problems, in 1958, the Chinese Government proclaimed that a combination of the pronunciation used by the people of Beijing and other northern cities become the standard speech of China. This is called Pǔtōnghuà [普通話]—literally *common speech*—and is referred to as 'Mandarin' by Westerners. Pǔtōnghuà (also called Hànyǔ [漢語]—*the language of the Han people*) is now the language taught at school, used on TV and radio, and in all official documents.

3 The writing

Chinese is the oldest living language. It is believed that the history of Chinese writing spans over 5,000 or 6,000 years. The earliest writings discovered, dated between 1480 BC and 1122 BC, are inscribed on oracle bones and turtle shells, and are called jiǎgǔwén [甲骨文]. These writings are the records of kings in the Shang dynasty who asked the gods about their fortune for hunting, going to war or any important event.

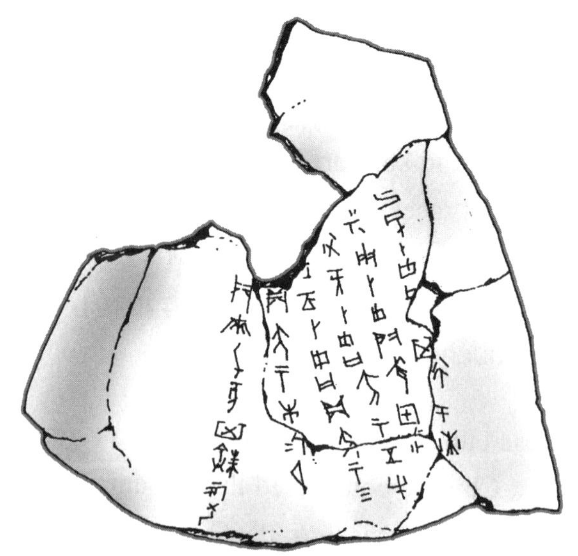

Some Chinese writing was developed from simple pictures taken from nature, such as animals, birds, mountains and rivers. The style of writing was changed several times and gradually transformed into the characters used today.

	sun	moon	mountain	tree	water	fire	person	mouth
picture								
early writing								
seal form								
modern form	日	月	山	木	水	火	人	口
Pinyin	rì	yuè	shān	mù	shuǐ	huǒ	rén	kǒu

Each Chinese character is pronounced as a single syllable and has its own meanings. Many ideas, thoughts and feelings are expressed by combining two or more simple characters to form a new character with a new meaning.

日 sun	+	月 moon	=	明 bright (míng)
木 tree	+	木 tree	=	林 forest (lín)
火 fire	+	火 fire	=	炎 hot (yán)

Two or more characters can also be used together to form a further meaning, but they remain separate characters.

火 fire	followed by	山 mountain	forms	火山 volcano (huǒshān)
山 mountain	followed by	水 water	forms	山水 scenery (shānshuǐ)
口 mouth	followed by	水 water	forms	口水 saliva (kǒushuǐ)
人 people	followed by	口 mouth	forms	人口 population (rénkǒu)

As Chinese writing is pictographic, some characters are complicated. In 1956, the Chinese Government began simplifying the structure of some characters to make them easier to write.

dragon	traditional	龍	>	simplified	龙	(lóng)
to study	traditional	學	>	simplified	学	(xué)
country	traditional	國	>	simplified	国	(guó)
happy	traditional	歡	>	simplified	欢	(huān)

These simplified characters have been widely and officially used in China ever since. Students learn the simplified form at school and all publications in China use the simplified form. However, most people in overseas Chinese communities and the people of Taiwan still use the traditional style, which is the style used in this edition.

The principles of writing the strokes in a Chinese character are basically from left to right, top to bottom, a tick and a hook. The character yǒng [永] (forever) is a good example to show the writing structure as it has many of the typical strokes used in most Chinese characters. Writing the strokes in the correct way, and in the correct order, is the first step to writing Chinese successfully.

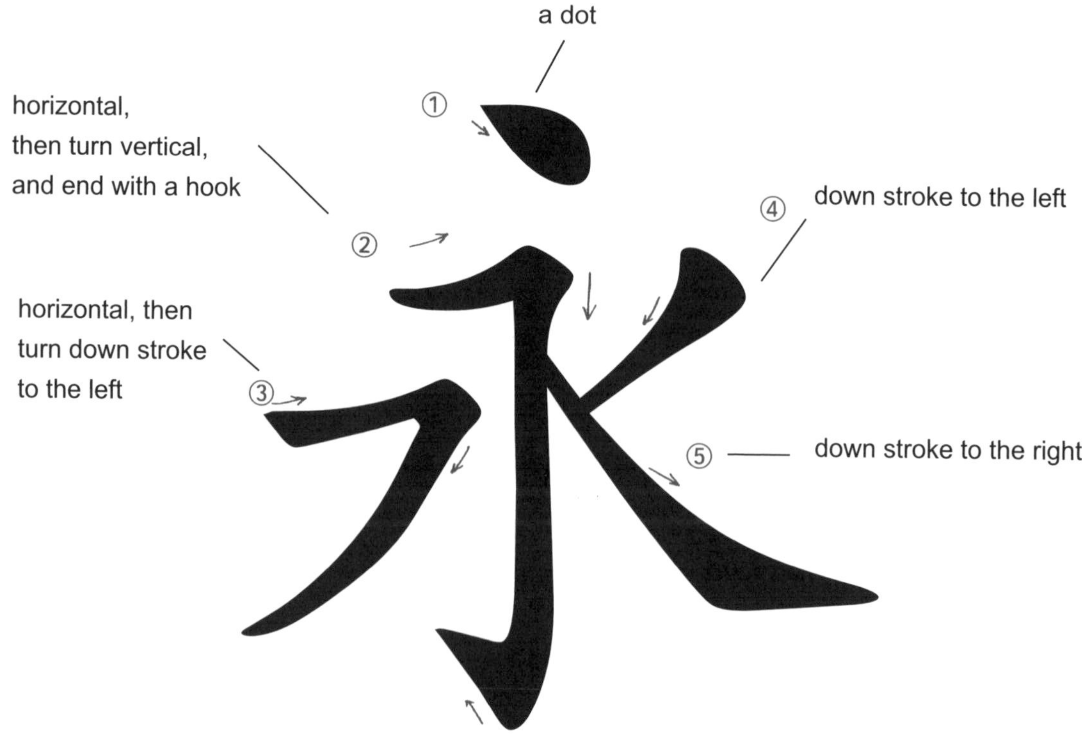

Chinese books are traditionally written from top to bottom, right to left, and bound with the spine on the right-hand side. In China today, publications, except calligraphy which still follows this tradition, are usually printed in the style used in the West. However, in Taiwan most newspapers, literary works and many other publications are still presented in the traditional style.

4 Pronunciation

As Chinese had no symbols to represent the sound of the words, in 1918 the Government of the Republic of China proclaimed thirty-nine symbols to represent the sounds. These phonetic symbols, i.e. ㄅㄆㄇㄈ... were named zhùyīn fúhào [注音符號] in 1930 and thirty-seven of them are still in use in Taiwan and many Chinese communities overseas. As these symbols are not easy to learn, Westerners have adopted various ways of using Roman letters, such as the Wade-Giles system and the Yale system, to represent each Chinese sound. In 1958, the Government of the People's Republic of China introduced another Romanization system, called *Pinyin* [拼音 pīnyīn]. Pinyin is now used in China and is an international system to express the sounds of the Chinese language as well as to spell Chinese names and places. The Pinyin system contains:

Initials		b	p	m	f		d	t	n	l
		g	k	h			j	q	x	
		zh	ch	sh	r		z	c	s	
		(y)	(w)							
Vowels	single	a	o	e	i	u	ü			
	double	ai	ei	ui	ao	ou	iu	ie	üe	er
	nasal	an	en	in	un	ün				
		ang	eng	ing	ong					
Special sounds		zhi	chi	shi	ri	zi	ci	si		
		yi	wu	yu						
		ye	yue	yin						
		yun	yuan	ying						

The pronunciation of the letters in the Pinyin system is somewhat different from that of English. Modern Chinese has 430 sounds, far less than the number of characters, therefore many characters share the same sound. The use of tone (pitch) is an important way to tell the differences in meaning of the same sound. There are four tones in the Chinese language.

ˉ	1st tone:	high level pitch
ˊ	2nd tone:	rising in pitch
ˇ	3rd tone:	low dipping pitch
ˋ	4th tone:	abrupt falling in pitch

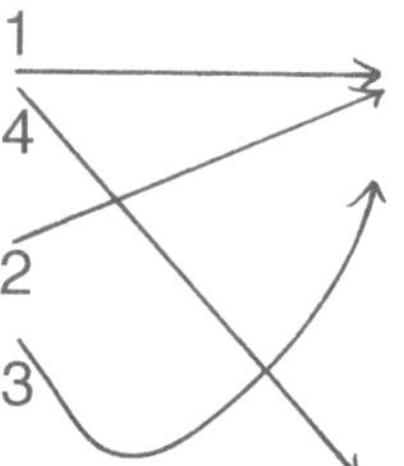

A change of tone will change the meaning of a sound. For example:

媽 mā	means	mother	八 bā	means	eight
麻 má	means	flax	拔 bá	means	to pull
馬 mǎ	means	horse	靶 bǎ	means	target
罵 mà	means	to scold	爸 bà	means	father

Many characters with different meanings also share the same sound and the same tone. For example:

梅 méi—plum　　眉 méi—eyebrow　　煤 méi—coal

In addition to the four tones there is a neutral tone that does not carry any tone mark. Sometimes the second character of a two-character word uses a neutral tone. Some words that have only grammatical function also use a neutral tone. For example:

爸爸 bàba—father　　媽媽 māma—mother　　鼻子 bízi—nose
好嗎？ Hǎo ma?—OK?　　好啊。 Hǎo a.—OK.　　太好了！ Tài hǎo le!—Great!

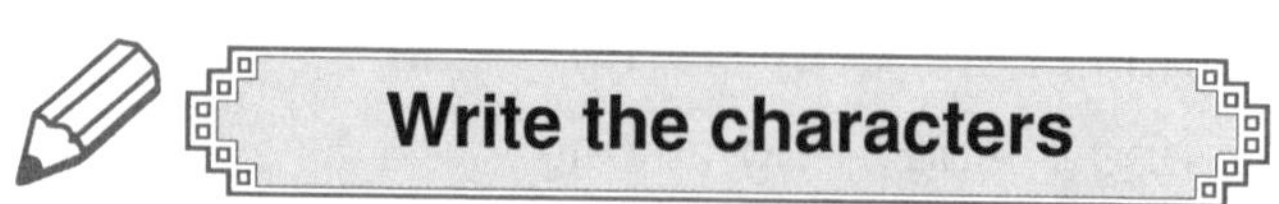

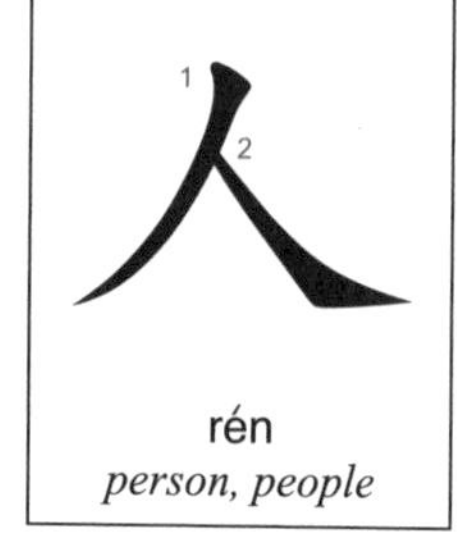

rén
person, people

shān
mountain

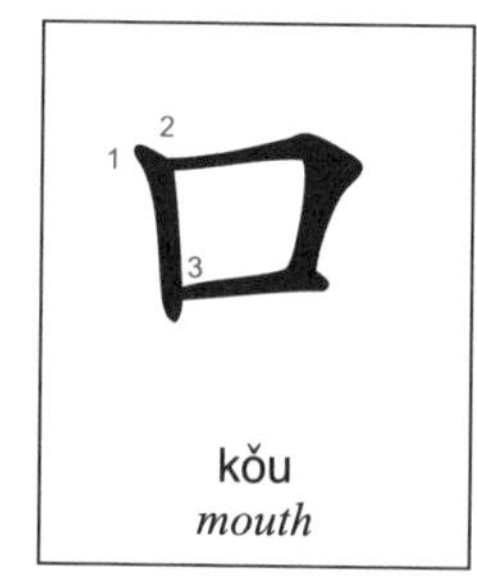

kǒu
mouth

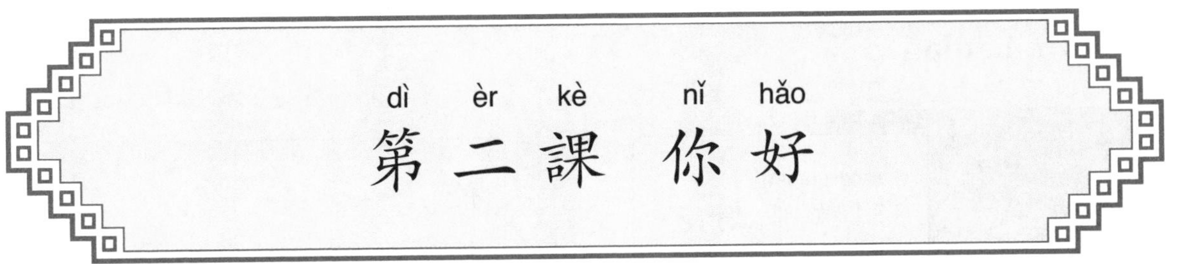

dì èr kè nǐ hǎo
第二課 你好

1 Hello!

2 I am Lanlan

tóngxuémen
同學們好。
Lín lǎoshī
林老師好。

你是……？
Lǐ Lánlán
我是李蘭蘭。
tā Bái Dàwěi
他是白大偉。

tóngxuémen zàijiàn
同學們再見。
lǎoshī
老師再見。

3 Good morning

Learn the sentences

In this section you will learn to use sentences. Have a conversation with your partner to practice the sentence patterns.

Greeting people

The most common way to greet people is to say nǐ hǎo 你好, or if it is early in the morning, zǎo 早. Chinese people often say nǐ hǎo 你好 to each other at any time of the day or when they are introduced to each other.

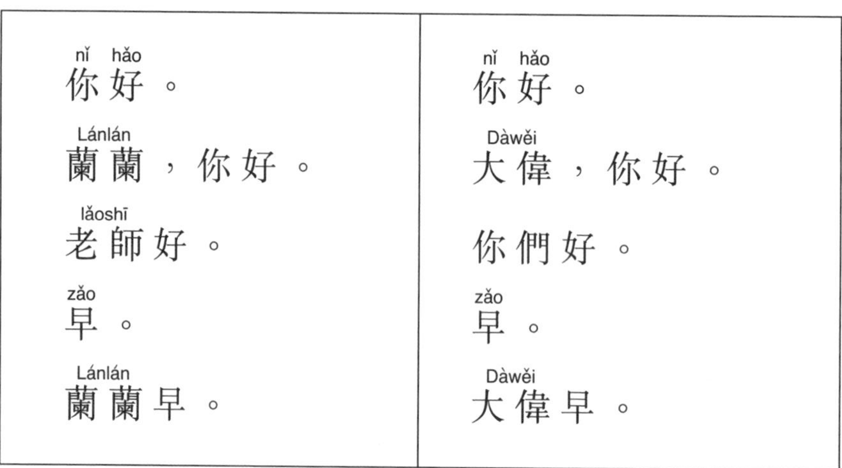

nǐ hǎo 你好。	nǐ hǎo 你好。
Lánlán 蘭蘭，你好。	Dàwěi 大偉，你好。
lǎoshī 老師好。	你們好。
zǎo 早。	zǎo 早。
Lánlán 蘭蘭早。	Dàwěi 大偉早。

Introducing

To introduce yourself, or to state someone's name, the verb shì 是 is used whether the subject is wǒ 我, nǐ 你 or tā 他.

你是……？	Lǐ Lánlán 我是李蘭蘭。
	Lín 我是林老師。
他是……？	Bái Dàwěi 他是白大偉。
	他是李老師。

Saying goodbye

To say goodbye, say zàijiàn 再見. To say see you tomorrow, say míngtiān jiàn 明天見. The person's name or title can also be said before or after zàijiàn 再見 or míngtiān jiàn 明天見.

zàijiàn 再見。	zàijiàn 再見。
míngtiān jiàn 明天見。	míngtiān jiàn 明天見。
tóngxuémen 同學們再見。	lǎoshī 老師再見。
明天見，蘭蘭。	明天見，大偉。

New words and expressions

你好	nǐ hǎo	hello, how do you do
你	nǐ	you (singular)
好	hǎo	good, well
我	wǒ	I, me
是	shì	am, is, are
白	Bái	a family name bái- white
大偉	Dàwěi	Chinese for David dà- big; wěi- great
李	Lǐ	a family name lǐ- plum
蘭蘭	Lánlán	a Chinese given name lán- orchid
再見	zàijiàn	goodbye zài- again; jiàn- to see
同學	tóngxué	fellow student, schoolmate tóng- same, together; xué- to learn
們	men	[used after a pronoun or a noun associated with people to show plural i.e. wǒmen 我們 – we; tāmen 他們 – they]
同學們	tóngxuémen	fellow students (plural of tóngxué 同學)
林	Lín	a family name lín- forest
老師	lǎoshī	teacher lǎo- old; shī- teacher
他	tā	he, him
早	zǎo	morning, early
你們	nǐmen	you (plural)
明天	míngtiān	tomorrow míng- tomorrow, bright; tiān- day
見	jiàn	to see

Write the characters

nǐ
you

hǎo
good

wǒ
I, me

shì
am, is, are

tā
he, him

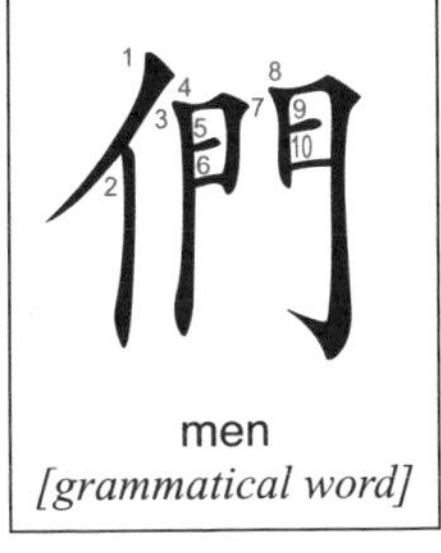

men
[grammatical word]

The character 們 contains elements of a standing person 亻 and a door 門. The standing person represents its meaning and the door (mén) represents its sound. 們 is used after a pronoun or a noun associated with people to indicate plural:

Singular		Plural
我	→	我們
你	→	你們
他	→	他們
同學	→	同學們

Something about characters

The Chinese consider a woman bearing a child (especially a son) to be good. The character 好 hǎo (good) in one of the early forms was written as [early form of 好], which is a combination of a kneeling woman [early form of 女] and a child [early form of 子].

Supplementary words and expressions

Classroom phrases

請進	qǐng jìn	come in please
請坐	qǐng zuò	sit down please
站起來	zhàn qǐlái	stand up
不要說話	bú yào shuōhuà	do not talk
注意聽	zhùyì tīng	listen carefully
請安靜	qǐng ānjìng	quiet please
看黑板	kàn hēibǎn	look at the blackboard
把書打開	bǎ shū dǎkāi	open (your) book
到前面來	dào qiánmiàn lái	come to the front
請回坐位	qǐng huí zuòwèi	return to (your) seat please
請坐好	qǐng zuò hǎo	sit properly please
請舉手	qǐng jǔshǒu	please raise (your) hand
把手放下	bǎ shǒu fàng xià	put down (your) hand
大聲一點	dà shēng yìdiǎn	a little louder
再說一次	zài shuō yí cì	say (it) again
很好	hěn hǎo	very good
非常好	fēicháng hǎo	extremely good

Something to know

Greetings

Nǐ hǎo 你好 is the most common greeting used by the Chinese. It is used at any time of the day or when people are introduced to each other. Other expressions used are:

Nǐ máng ma? [你忙嗎？] Are you busy?
Zěmeyàng? [怎麼樣？] How is everything?
Shàng nǎr qù? [上哪兒去？] Where are you going?
Chī fàn le ma? [吃飯了嗎？] Have you eaten?

These greetings show concern for each other. When asked where they are going, people do not feel that their private lives have been intruded upon and would happily answer 'going shopping', 'going to work', or other similar expressions.

Chinese names

In Chinese, the family name is placed first followed by the given name. Most names contain three characters: the first character is the family name and the following two are the given name. However, some people may have two characters for their family name or just one character for their given name.

When naming a newborn, most parents would choose Chinese characters that best express their expectations for that child, for example, Jiànxióng [健雄] (strong and brave), and Fāngfāng [芳芳] (fragrant).

Addressing teachers

Chinese students do not address their teachers as Mr, Mrs, Ms or Miss, instead they use their professional title, lǎoshī [老師] (teacher). They either address their teachers as lǎoshī, or say the family name followed by lǎoshī. For example, if the teacher's family name is Lín [林], they address him/her as Lín lǎoshī [林老師]; if the teacher's family name is Bái [白], they address him/her as Bái lǎoshī [白老師].

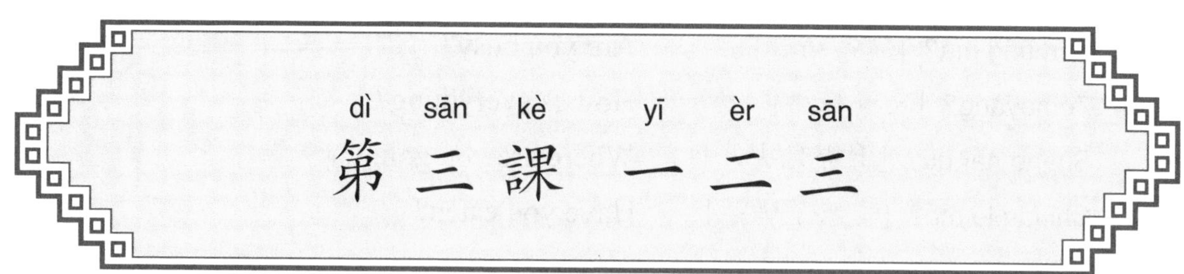

dì sān kè yī èr sān
第三課 一二三

1 Numbers up to 10

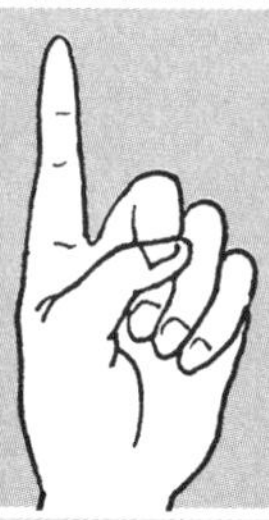

yī
一

èr
二

sān
三

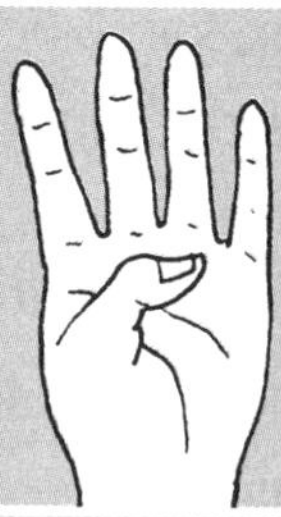

sì
四

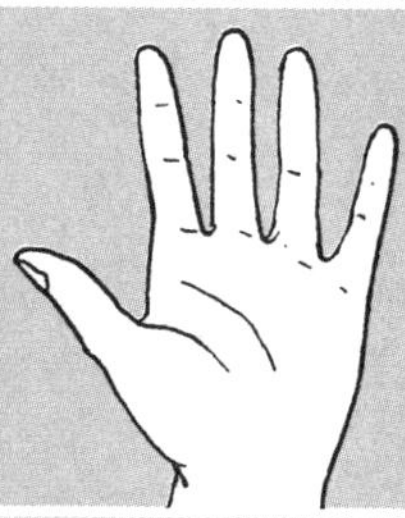

wǔ
五

liù
六

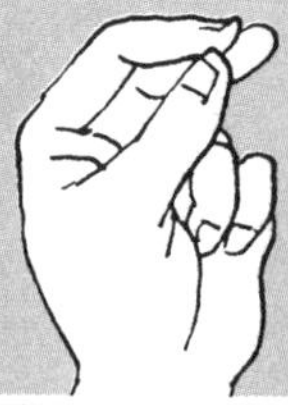

qī
七

bā
八

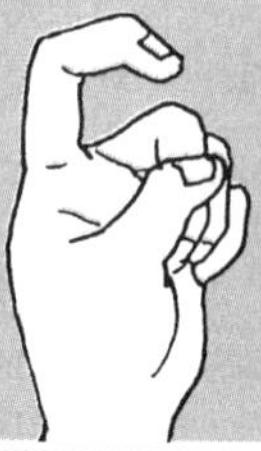

jiǔ
九

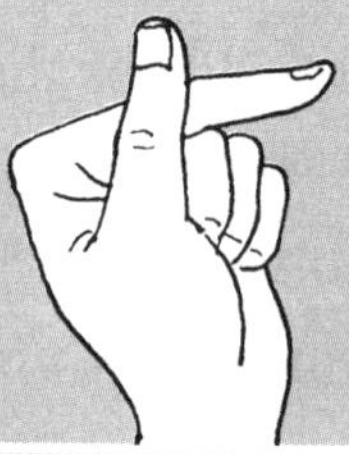

shí
十

一 二 三

líng
〇 = zero

一九〇五 = 1905

二〇〇一 = 2001

A tongue twister

三是三，山是山；

四是四，十是十。

2 Important numbers

3 Numbers 0 to 100

líng 〇	shí 十	èrshí 二十	sānshí 三十	sìshí 四十
一	十一	二十一	三十一	四十一
二	十二	二十二	三十二	四十二
三	十三	二十三	三十三	四十三
四	十四	二十四	三十四	四十四
五	十五	二十五	三十五	四十五
六	十六	二十六	三十六	四十六
七	十七	二十七	三十七	四十七
八	十八	二十八	三十八	四十八
九	十九	二十九	三十九	四十九

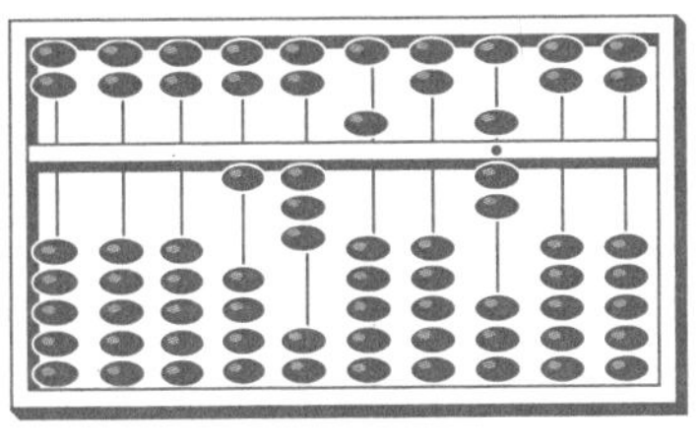

一三五〇七

wǔshí 五十	liùshí 六十	qīshí 七十	bāshí 八十	jiǔshí 九十	yìbǎi 一百
五十一	六十一	七十一	八十一	九十一	
五十二	六十二	七十二	八十二	九十二	
五十三	六十三	七十三	八十三	九十三	
五十四	六十四	七十四	八十四	九十四	
五十五	六十五	七十五	八十五	九十五	
五十六	六十六	七十六	八十六	九十六	
五十七	六十七	七十七	八十七	九十七	
五十八	六十八	七十八	八十八	九十八	
五十九	六十九	七十九	八十九	九十九	

4 Math quiz

5 ＋ 8 ＝ 13	jiā dĕngyú 五加八等於十三
69 － 5 ＝ 64	jiǎn dĕngyú 六十九減五等於六十四
8 × 7 ＝ 56	chéng yǐ dĕngyú 八乘以七等於五十六
27 ÷ 9 ＝ 3	chú yǐ dĕngyú 二十七除以九等於三

jiā chú yǐ
88 加 8，除以 8，
加 88

dĕngyú
等於 100

jiā
77 加 77，加 7，
chú yǐ
除以 7，加 77

dĕngyú
等於 100

chéng yǐ jiǎn
55 乘以 5，減 55，
jiā chú yǐ
加 5，除以 5，加 55

dĕngyú
等於……等於……

New words and expressions

一	yī	one
二	èr	two
三	sān	three
四	sì	four
五	wǔ	five
六	liù	six
七	qī	seven
八	bā	eight
九	jiǔ	nine
十	shí	ten
○	líng	zero
百	bǎi	hundred
加	jiā	plus, to add
等於	děngyú	to be equal to
減	jiǎn	minus, to subtract
乘以	chéng yǐ	multiplied by chéng- to multiply
除以	chú yǐ	divided by chú- to divide

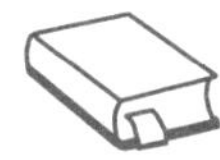

Supplementary words

Number Sequence

第一	dì yī	the first
第二	dì èr	the second
第三	dì sān	the third
……		
第一課	dì yī kè	lesson one
第二課	dì èr kè	lesson two
第三課	dì sān kè	lesson three
……		

Write the characters

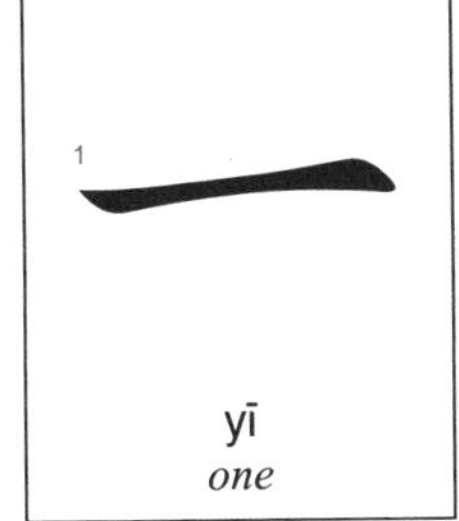

yī
one

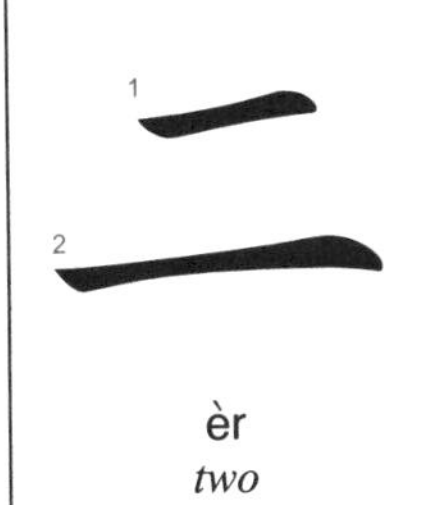

èr
two

sān
three

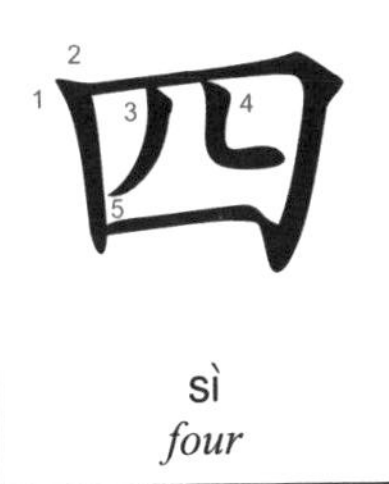

sì
four

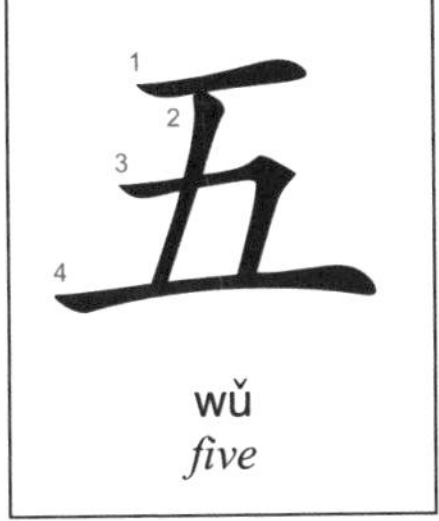

wǔ
five

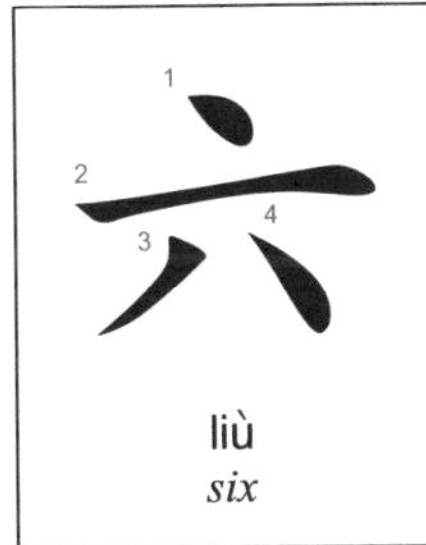

liù
six

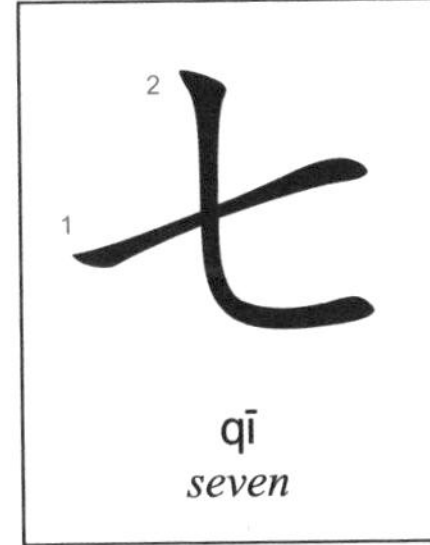

qī
seven

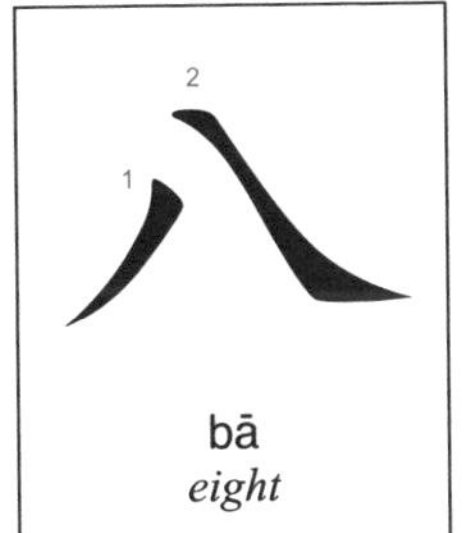

bā
eight

jiǔ
nine

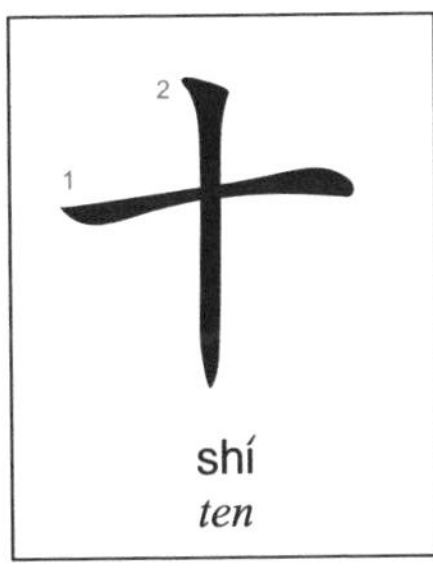

shí
ten

Something to know

Lucky and unlucky numbers

The Chinese like the concept of pairs, believing them auspicious for happy events. The symbol [囍] (shuāng xǐ, double happiness), is formed by joining two [喜] (xǐ, happiness), and is used during wedding ceremonies to wish couples happiness for the future.

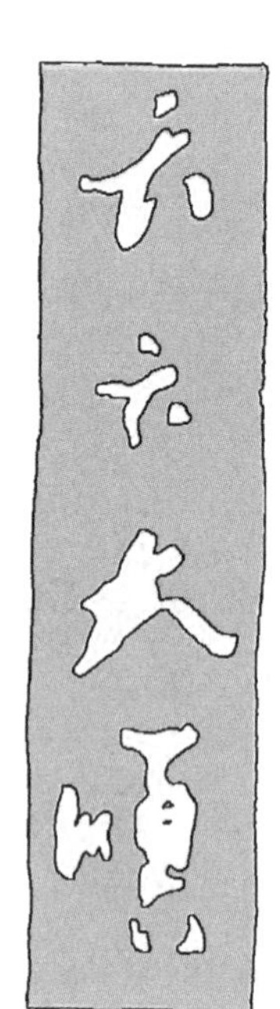

Five and six are also regarded as lucky numbers by Chinese, and are often used in phrases meaning lucky.

wǔ fú lín mén [五福臨門]	(the arrival of five happinesses)
liù liù dà shùn [六六大順]	(double lucky six)

Some people like to choose telephone numbers ending with double six hoping that it will bring them luck.

The number four—sì [四]—is generally regarded to be unlucky as it has the same pronunciation, although a different tone, as the word for death—sǐ [死].

People try to avoid using the number four for things associated with illness or danger. Some hospitals in Taiwan do not have a fourth floor as it would shock the patients' families to hear that their loved ones were on the 'death floor'. Some people also avoid car registration numbers ending in four. However, not all Chinese believe in this superstition, just as not all Westerners believe that the number thirteen is unlucky.

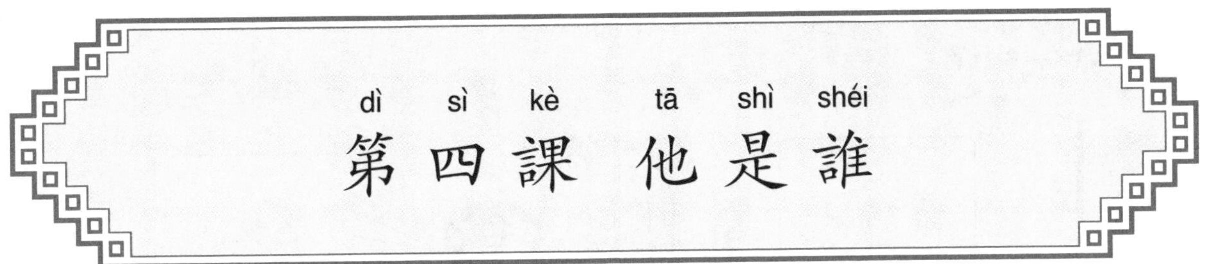

dì sì kè tā shì shéi
第四課 他是誰

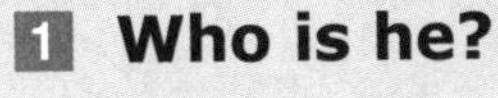

1 **Who is he?**

2 Who is it?

3 How old are you?

Learn the sentences

Identifying people

To ask Who is he/she? say Tā shì shéi? 他/她是誰? To answer the question, replace the question word shéi 誰 with the person's name. Note that the word order remains the same in both the question and the answer.

他是誰(shéi)？	他是大偉(Dàwěi)。 他是馬克(Mǎkè)。
她是誰？	她是林(Lín)老師(lǎoshī)。
你是誰？	我是蘭蘭(Lánlán)。

To find out who is at the door, Chinese often say Shéi a? 誰啊? To answer this question, say Shì wǒ. 是我。 or to be more polite, say your name.

誰啊(a)？	是我。 是我，蘭蘭(Lánlán)。 是我，白(Bái)大偉(Dàwěi)。

Asking about age

To ask a child How old are you? Chinese often say Nǐ jǐ suì? 你幾歲? To answer this question, replace jǐ 幾 with the age. The word order remains the same whether it is a question or an answer.

It is common in Chinese to add the word jīnnián 今年 to ask how old a person is this year, so people generally ask Nǐ jīnnián jǐ suì? 你今年幾歲? Note that jīnnián 今年 is not placed at the end of the sentence as this year is in English.

你幾(jǐ)歲(suì)？	我八歲(suì)。
他幾歲？	他三歲。
她幾歲？	她七歲。
你今年(jīnnián)幾歲？	我今年(jīnnián)十一歲。
他今年幾歲？	他今年兩(liǎng)歲。

New words and expressions

誰	shéi	who, whom [a question word]
馬克	Mǎkè	Chinese for Mark mǎ- horse; kè- to overcome
她	tā	she, her
啊	a	[an exclamation]
歡迎	huānyíng	welcome
請進	qǐng jìn	come in please qǐng- please; jìn- to come in
謝謝	xièxie	thanks
祝	zhù	to wish (offer good wishes)
生日	shēngrì	birthday shēng- to give birth to; rì- day, sun
快樂	kuàilè	happy kuài- happy, fast; lè- happy
今年	jīnnián	this year jīn- this, present (time); nián- year
幾	jǐ	how many
歲	suì	year of age
兩	liǎng	two (before measure words, age and some numerals)

Write the characters

shéi
who, whom

tā
she, her

lǎo
old

shī
teacher

jǐ
how many

suì
year of age

liǎng
two

Play school

Something about characters

Each Chinese character contains a basic element relating to the meaning of the character. This element is called the *'radical'*. Some characters only contain one element, that is, they are themselves radicals, such as 人 rén (people) and 山 shān (mountain). A great proportion of characters contain two elements with the radical indicating the meaning and the other element indicating the sound. For example, the character 他 tā (he), contains the radical for person 亻 and the character 她 tā (she), has the radical for woman 女. An old pronunciation of 也 in each character indicates the sound.

Chinese age

The Chinese use two methods of counting age: one is called shísuì [實歲]—full age; and the other is called xūsuì [虛歲]—function age. Generally, people use the xūsuì method. With this method children are considered to be one year old as soon as they are born, and two years old after New Year's Eve (Chinese lunar calendar). For example, a child born on New Year's Eve would be two years old on New Year's Day.

How old are you?

Nǐ jǐ suì? [你幾歲？] is the most common way to ask a child his/her age. Sometimes the Chinese also use Nǐ duó dà? [你多大？].

In Western society, adults—especially women—do not like being asked about their age, and it is considered impolite to ask an adult's age. In Chinese society, it is common for adults to ask each other's age and this is not regarded as improper. However, they do not normally ask the other's age directly, but ask the year in which he/she was born and then work out the age for themselves. The questions asked are:

> Nǐ shì nǎ nián shēng de? [你是哪年生的？] In which year were you born?
> Nǐ shǔ shéme? [你屬什麼？] In what animal year were you born?

Many elderly Chinese enjoy being asked their age as they believe it shows the questioner's respect for their experience, knowledge and health. People normally use questions such as:

> Nín duó dà niánjì? [您多大年紀？] (literally—*How big is your age?*)
> Nín gāo shòu? [您高壽？] (literally—*Your high age?*)

Nín [您] is the polite form of nǐ [你]. Older people, who are usually very proud of their age, would be happy to tell the questioner how old they are.

Birthdays

In the past, it was uncommon for the Chinese to celebrate their children's birthdays every year. However, due to the influence of Western ideas, some parents have begun to celebrate their children's birthdays with a birthday cake.

Traditionally, the Chinese celebrate the birth of their children—especially their sons—after the first month, and after the first year. Boiled eggs colored red are given to friends and relatives when the baby is one month old, and a party is held when the baby is one year old. Children's birthdays are then normally ignored.

After the first birthday, the next important birthday celebration is at thirty years old and then at forty, fifty, sixty and so on. The older the person becomes, the bigger the celebration. The word shòu [壽] (longevity) is used in a variety of styles at such celebrations to wish the person a long life.

During the birthday party, steamed buns in the shape of a peach, which symbolize long life, called shòutáo [壽桃], are distributed. Noodles that also symbolize long life, called shòumiàn [壽麵], are eaten. In Taiwan, guests are offered boiled pig's leg with noodles, called zhūjiǎo miànxiàn [豬腳麵線]. When eating the noodles, which are usually long, the guests should be careful not to break the noodles as they represent the long life of the person celebrating his/her birthday.

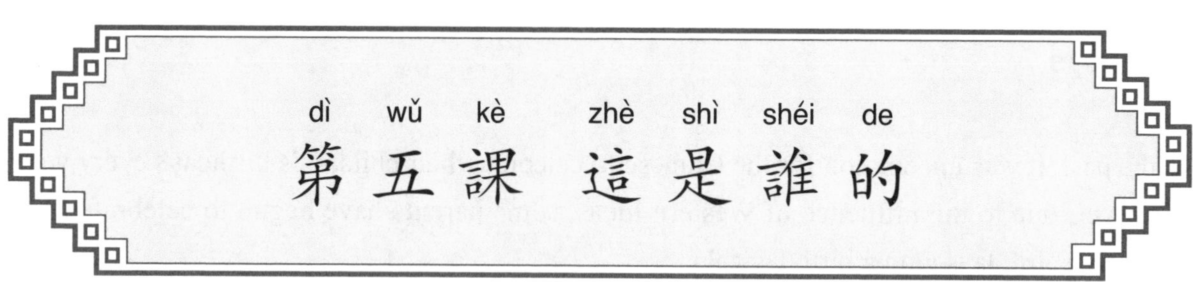

dì wǔ kè zhè shì shéi de
第五課 這是誰的

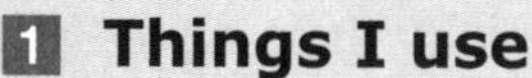

1 Things I use

chǐ
尺

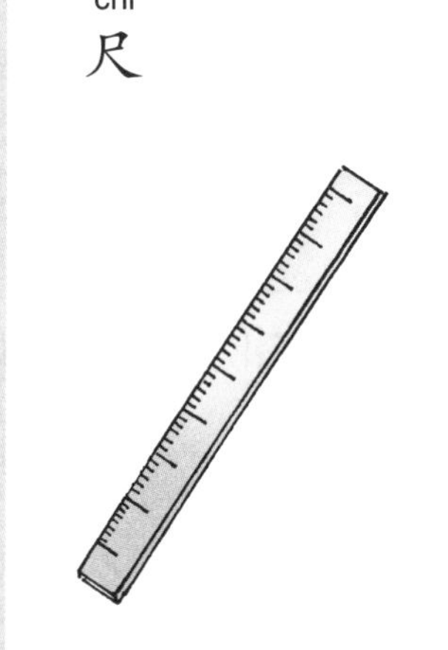

jiǎndāo
剪刀

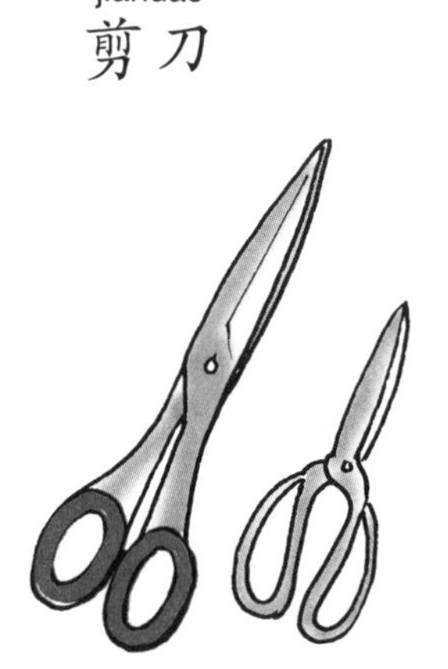

bǐ
筆

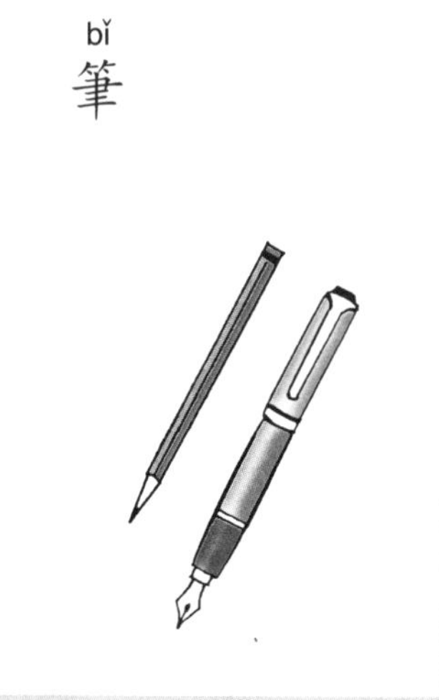

shū
書

máobǐ
毛筆

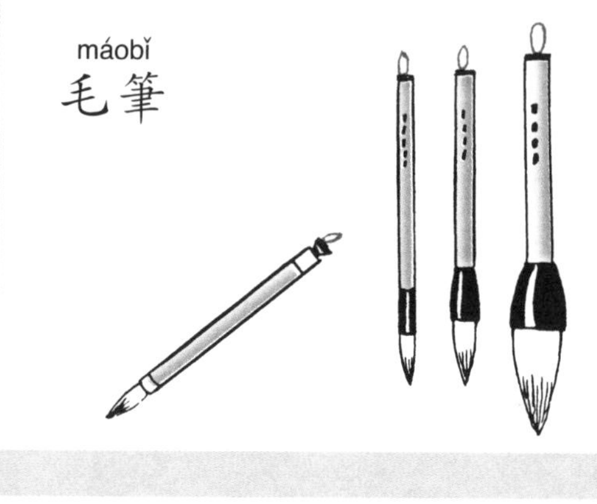

shūbāo
書包

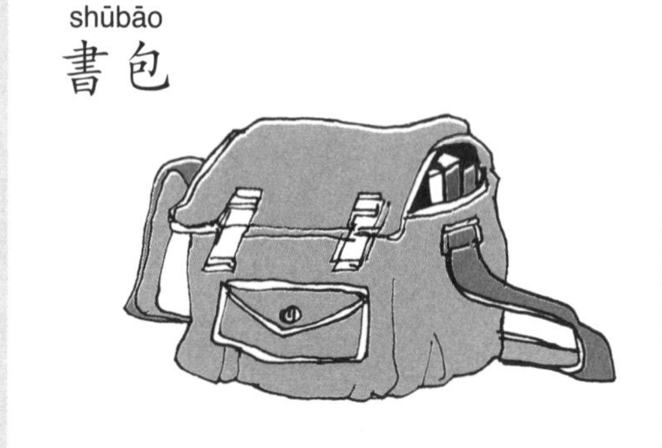

xiàngpí
橡皮

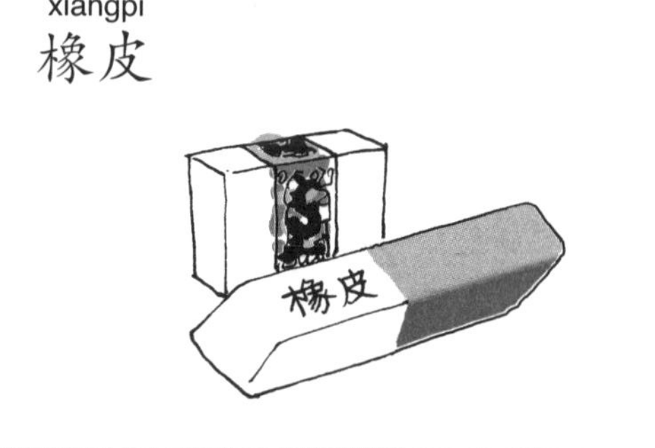

2 What is this?

3 Whose is this?

4 Is this yours?

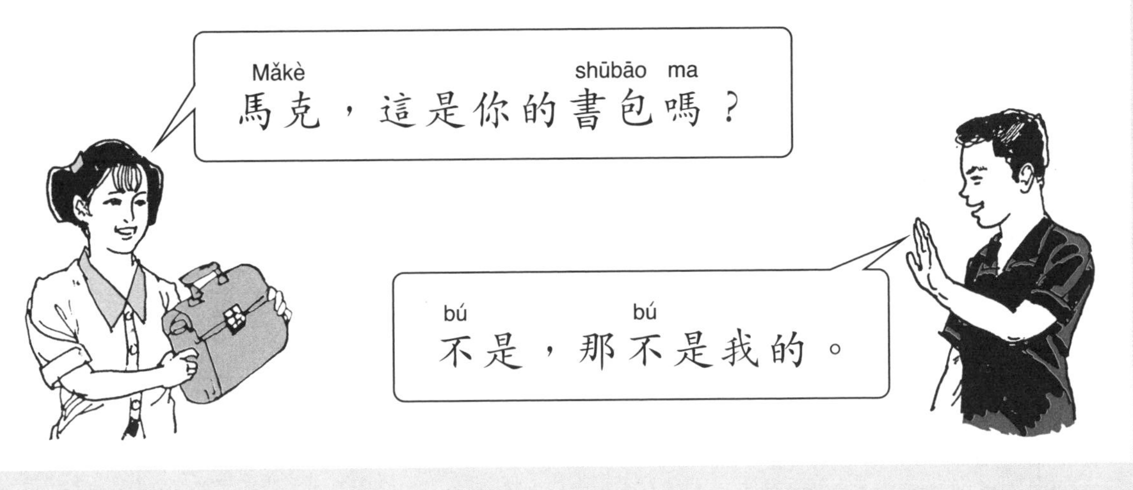

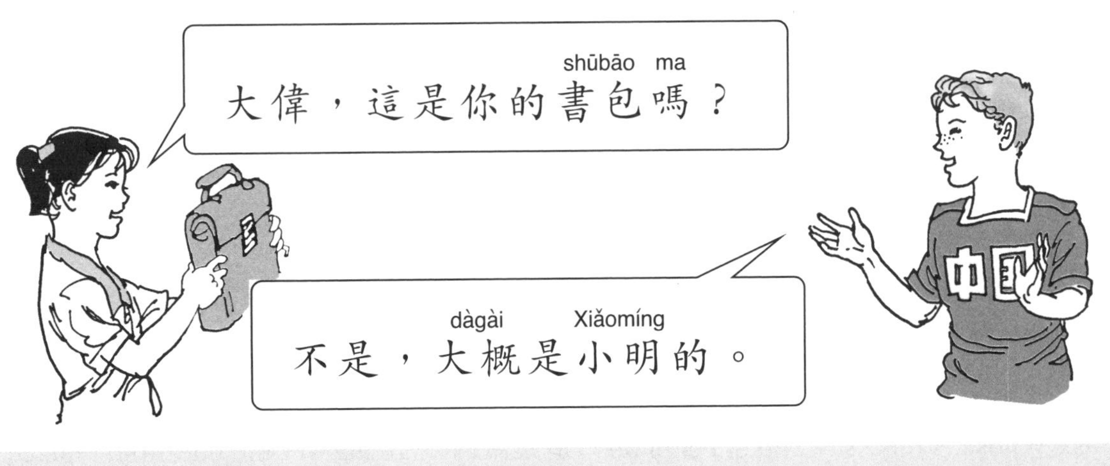

Learn the sentences

Identifying objects

To ask What is this? say Zhè shì shéme? 這是什麼? To answer the question, replace the question word shéme 什麼 with the object.

zhè shéme 這 是 什 麼 ？	jiǎndāo 這 是 剪 刀 。 xiàngpí 這 是 橡 皮 。
nà shéme 那 是 什 麼 ？	chǐ 那 是 尺 。 máobǐ 那 是 毛 筆 。

Asking who owns an object

To ask Whose is this? say Zhè shì shéi de? 這是誰的? To answer the question, replace the question word shéi 誰 with the owner.

de 這 是 誰 的 ？	這 是 我 的 。
那 是 誰 的 ？	Lánlán 那 是 蘭 蘭 的 。
shū 這 是 誰 的 書 ？	shū 這 是 老 師 的 書 。 Dàwěi 這 是 大 偉 的 。
bǐ 那 是 誰 的 筆 ？	Xiǎomíng bǐ 那 是 小 明 的 筆 。 那 是 我 的 。

Asking if things belong to someone

To say This is your book. say Zhè shì nǐ de shū. 這是你的書。To ask Is this your book? say Zhè shì nǐ de shū ma? 這是你的書嗎?

The first statement was changed into a question by adding the question word ma 嗎 at the end. This is one way to turn a statement into a question where the answer can be yes or no.

Chinese answer yes to a question by repeating the verb and answer no by saying the negative form of the verb used in the question. The negative form of shì 是 is búshì 不是. For yes, shìde 是的 is sometimes used instead of shì 是, as it sounds better.

shūbāo ma 這是你的書包嗎?	是,這是我的。 bú 不是,這不是我的。
máobǐ 那是你的毛筆嗎?	是的,那是我的。 不是,那不是我的。

Asking if someone knows something

To ask Do you know? say Nǐ zhīdào ma? 你知道嗎? To answer yes, repeat the verb in the question, i.e. zhīdào 知道. To answer no, add the negative word bù 不 in front of the verb, i.e. bù zhīdào 不知道.

zhīdào 你知道嗎?	zhīdào 我知道。 bù 我不知道。
他知道嗎?	他知道。 他不知道。

New words and expressions

誰的	shéi de	whose　shéi- who
尺	chǐ	ruler
剪刀	jiǎndāo	scissors　jiǎn- to cut; dāo- knife
筆	bǐ	pen
書	shū	book
毛筆	máobǐ	writing brush　máo- fur, feather, wool; bǐ- pen
書包	shūbāo	school bag　shū- book; bāo- bag
橡皮	xiàngpí	eraser　xiàng- rubber tree; pí- skin, leather
這	zhè	this
什麼	shéme	what
不	bù	no, not (used to form negative) —tone changes to second when followed by a fourth tone, e.g. bú shì 不是
知道	zhīdào	to know
嗎	ma	[a question word]
那	nà	that
的	de	[a possessive particle used after the pronoun or noun]
我的	wǒ de	my, mine
大概	dàgài	probably　dà- big; gài- approximate
你的	nǐ de	your, yours
不是	bú shì	no (negative form of shì 是)
小明	Xiǎomíng	a Chinese given name　xiǎo- small, little; míng- bright
是的	shìde	yes (positive answer to questions using the verb shì 是)
不客氣	bú kèqì	not at all, don't mention it, you're welcome　bù, bú- no, not; kèqì- polite
和	hé, hàn	and

Supplementary words

Nouns for students

教室	jiàoshì	classroom	椅子	yǐzi	chair
門	mén	door	鉛筆	qiānbǐ	pencil
窗户	chuānghù	window	鉛筆盒	qiānbǐhé	pencil case
黑板	hēibǎn	blackboard	原子筆	yuánzǐbǐ	ball-point pen
黑板擦	hēibǎncā	blackboard eraser	膠水	jiāoshuǐ	glue
粉筆	fěnbǐ	chalk	彩色筆	cǎisèbǐ	color pencil
桌子	zhuōzi	desk	紙	zhǐ	paper

Write the characters

zhè
this

那
nà
that

什
shé
what

me
[word ending]

ma
[question word]

de
[possessive particle]

bù
not

'Found and Lost'

A rhyme

一 二 三 、 三 二 一 ，

chǐ　jiǎndāo　shū　hé　bǐ

尺 、 剪 刀 、 書 和 筆 ；

一 二 三 四 五 六 七 ，

máobǐ　shūbāo　hé　xiàngpí

毛 筆 、 書 包 和 橡 皮 。

Something to know

The finger-guessing game

Chinese children often use ‘finger-guessing’ to decide what game to play or who will be the first player in a game. This finger-guessing game is called cāiquán [猜拳]—guess the fist. The players thrust out a hand in one of three ways: scissors, stone or cloth. Jiǎndāo [剪刀] (scissors) is formed by extending and separating the index and middle fingers. Shítóu [石頭] (stone) is formed by making a fist and bù [布] (cloth) is formed by an open hand. The winner is:

scissors	cut	cloth	=	scissors win
cloth	wraps	stone	=	cloth wins
stone	breaks	scissors	=	stone wins

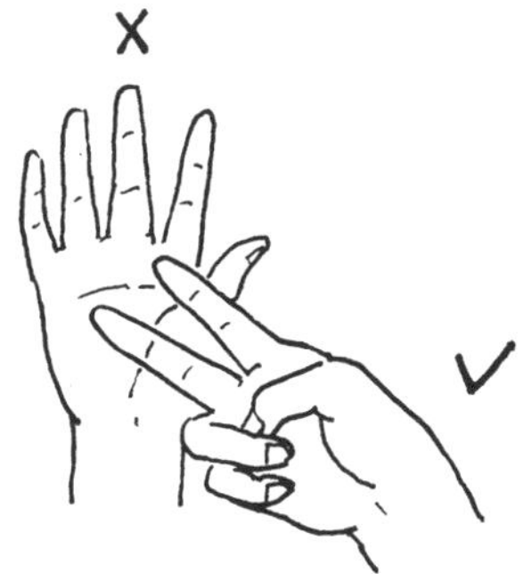

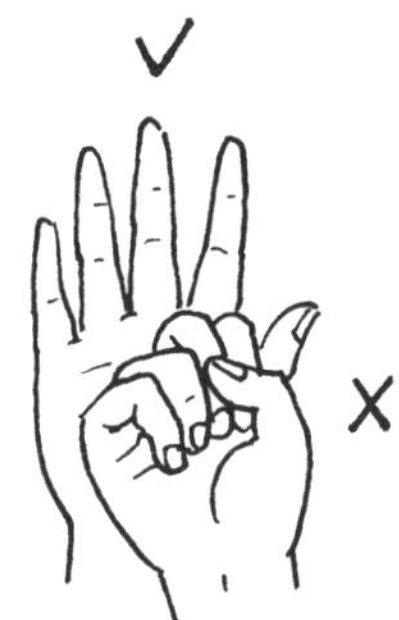

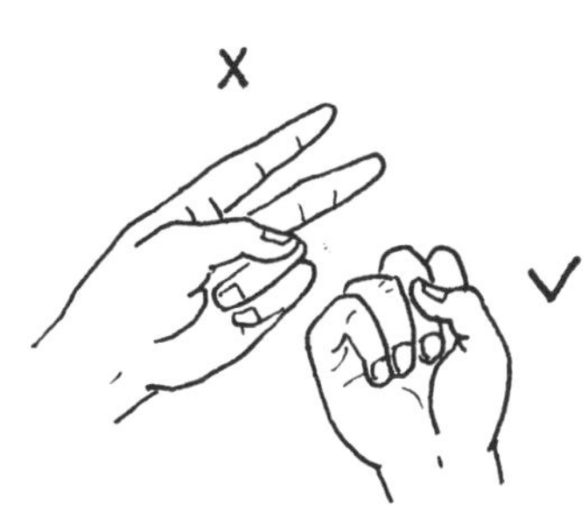

When playing the finger-guessing game, the players usually chant jiǎndāo 剪刀、shítóu 石頭、bù 布 and thrust out their hands, or alternatively say 一、二、三.

Calligraphy

Shūfǎ [書法] (calligraphy) is a Chinese art. Most Chinese artists are skilled in both calligraphy and painting as they are related art forms. The Chinese believe that an artist should be a master of the brush and should be able to write well.

The four traditional tools for calligraphy are the máobǐ [毛筆] (brush), the mò [墨] (ink-stick), the zhǐ [紙] (paper), and the yàntái [硯台] (ink-stone). The ink-stick is ground on the ink-stone with a little water to make ink. To save time, many people nowadays use bottled ink instead. Good calligraphy is treasured as much as a good painting. People frame and hang calligraphy on their walls to appreciate and admire it as they would a painting.

Early Chinese inventions

Paper, gunpowder and the compass are the three most commonly known Chinese inventions. Chinese first used silk floss then linen pulp to make paper. In 105 AD, Cài Lún [蔡倫] further improved the technique by pounding bark, linen scraps and old fish nets into a pulp which was spread to form paper. This 'Cai Lun' paper was then popularly used. Gunpowder was invented by Chinese between 220 and 280 AD. By the 10th century, the use of gunpowder was common. However, gunpowder was first used to power rockets and firecrackers rather than for military, engineering or mining purposes. It was more than 2,000 years ago when the earth's magnetism was observed by the Chinese and a magnetized needle device was developed in the 11th century.

China has the longest history of producing silk and its exporting of silk formed 'silk roads' to the West and to northeast Asia. Bì Shēng [畢昇] invented moveable type for printing in the 11th century, around 400 years before Gutenberg's printing of the Latin Bible in the West. It was also recorded that Chinese used a silver-tin amalgam to fill holes in teeth over one thousand years ago.

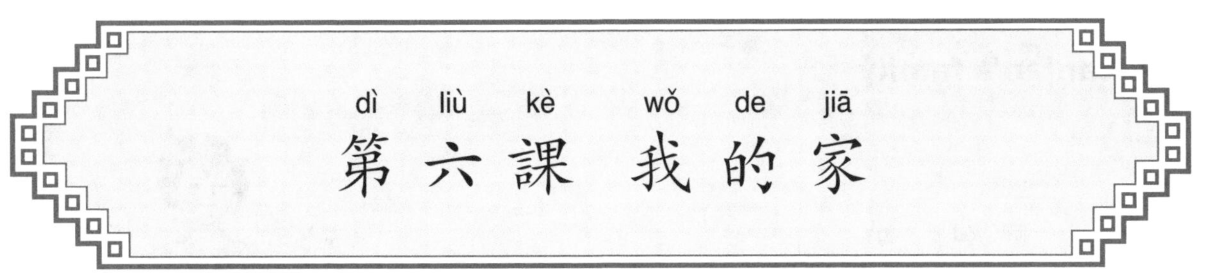

1 My family

我的家

adapted from 〈妹妹抱著洋娃娃〉

2 Lanlan's family

jiā yǒu ge
我家有三個人。

這是我的爸爸。
jīnnián
他今年四十五歲。
gōngrén
他是工人。

這是我媽媽。
jīnnián
她今年三十八歲。
hùshì
她是護士。

這是我。
jīnnián
我今年十二歲。
xuéshēng
我是學生。

3 David's family

你好。

xìng Bái　　jiào Bái Dàwěi
我姓白，我叫白大偉。

我家有五個人。

yīshēng
我爸爸是醫生。

我媽媽是老師。

我有一個哥哥，一個妹妹。

jiào Bǎoluó
我哥哥叫保羅 (Paul)。

jiào Lìlì
我妹妹叫麗麗 (Lily)。

4 Do you have any brothers or sisters?

ne
我家有三個人，你家呢？

我家有五個人。

你有哥哥嗎？

有，我有一個哥哥。

你有姊姊嗎？

méi
沒有，我沒有姊姊。

你有弟弟、妹妹嗎？

我沒有弟弟；
我有一個妹妹。

Learn the sentences

Asking about family

English sometimes uses words to state the number of things, for example, a piece of paper, a loaf of bread, a pair of shoes. Chinese, however, needs a measure word for everything, even people. The common measure word used for people is ge 個. To say one person, say yí ge rén 一個人.

To ask How many people are there in your family? say Nǐ jiā yǒu jǐ ge rén? 你家有幾個人? To answer the question, replace jǐ 幾 with the number of people.

jiā yǒu ge 你家有幾個人？	我家有三個人。 我家有五個人。
他家有幾個人？	他家有七個人。 他家有六個人。

Stating occupation

To state someone's occupation, use the verb shì 是 followed by the occupation. To say He is a doctor. say Tā shì yīshēng. 他是醫生。

yīshēng 他是醫生。
xuéshēng 我是學生。
gōngrén 我爸爸是工人。
我哥哥是老師。

Asking someone's name

To ask What is your name? say Nǐ jiào shéme míngzi? 你叫什麼名字？ To tell someone your family name, say wǒ xìng 我姓 followed by your family name. To tell someone your full name or just your given name, say wǒ jiào 我叫 followed by your full name or your given name. Remember, when saying your full name, always say your family name first and then your given name.

jiào míngzi 你叫什麼名字？	xìng Bái jiào Dàwěi 我姓白，叫白大偉。 Lǐ Lánlán 我姓李，叫李蘭蘭。 Bǎoluó 我叫白保羅。 Lìlì 我叫麗麗。

Asking about brothers and sisters

To ask Do you have any elder brothers? say Nǐ yǒu gēge ma? 你有哥哥嗎？ The same pattern is used to ask about elder sisters, younger brothers and younger sisters.

We learned in lesson five that to answer yes to this type of question, repeat the verb, which in this example is yǒu 有. To answer no, use the negative form of the verb. The negative word used for yǒu 有 is méi 沒, so the answer to this question is either yǒu 有 or méi yǒu 沒有.

你有哥哥嗎？	有，我有兩個哥哥。 méi 沒有，我沒有哥哥。
你有妹妹嗎？	有，我有一個妹妹。 我沒有妹妹。

New words and expressions

家	jiā	family, home
爸爸	bàba	dad, father
媽媽	māma	mom, mother
哥哥	gēge	elder brother
姊姊	jiějie	elder sister
弟弟	dìdi	younger brother
妹妹	mèimei	younger sister
有	yǒu	to have, there is/are
個	ge	[a common measure word which can be used for people]
也	yě	also, too
工人	gōngrén	laborer, worker gōng- work; rén- person, people
護士	hùshì	nurse hù- to nurse; shì- a person trained in a certain field
學生	xuéshēng	student, pupil xué- to learn, to study; shēng- pupil, student, person
姓	xìng	family name, surname
叫	jiào	to be called, to call
醫生	yīshēng	doctor yī- to cure; shēng- pupil, student, person
保羅	Bǎoluó	Chinese for Paul bǎo- to keep; luó- to collect
麗麗	Lìlì	Chinese for Lily lì- beautiful
呢	ne	(a question word) how about, e.g. nǐ ne 你呢? – how about you?
		nǐ jiā ne 你家呢? – how about your family?
沒	méi	(a negative word)
沒有	méi yǒu	not have
名字	míngzi	name

Write the characters

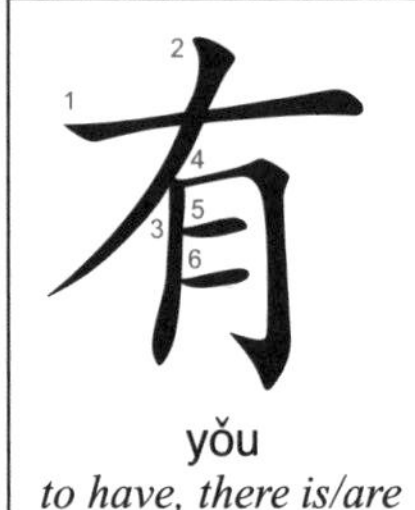

Supplementary words

More about the family

爺爺	yéye	granddad, grandfather
奶奶	nǎinai	grandma, grandmother
繼父	jìfù	stepfather
繼母	jìmǔ	stepmother
伯伯	bóbo	father's elder brother
叔叔	shúshu	father's younger brother (pronounced as shūshu in China)
舅舅	jiùjiu	mother's brother
姑姑	gūgu	father's sister
阿姨	āyí	mother's sister (said as yí 姨 in China)
丈夫	zhàngfū	husband
妻子	qīzi	wife
先生	xiānshēng	Mr, also used as husband
太太	tàitai	Mrs, also used as wife
兒子	érzi	son
女兒	nǚ'ér	daughter

Not what it seems

Family size

Traditionally, the Chinese had big families. Three or four generations, including brothers' and cousins' families, usually all lived together in one large house. However, this situation has changed dramatically since the beginning of the 20th century. Small families made up of parents and their unmarried children have become more and more common.

The large family tradition was further shattered in the 1970s when the *one family, one child policy* was introduced. People used to like having many children, especially sons to carry on the family name and to help with work. The policy, aiming to reduce the population growth, was strictly practiced and as a result, a great proportion of families have been down-sized to three members. Although a change to this policy in 2000 has allowed some families to have two children, it only applies to families where both husband and wife are from single child families.

Something about characters

Long ago, pigs were considered to be important family members as they represented the wealth of the family. The early form of the character 家 jiā (family or home), was written as 家 which is a pig 豕 under a shelter 宀.

The character 媽 mā (mother) has the radical for woman 女 nǚ, while the character 嗎 ma (a question word) has the radical for mouth 口 kǒu. Both these characters take their sound, but in different tones, from the element horse 馬 mǎ.

Addressing family members

In the traditional large Chinese family, a system based on respect has been developed to keep the family in harmony. Under this system, one does not call older members of the family by their given names but uses forms of address or titles instead.

The forms of address used are more complicated than those used in Western countries. The brothers of both parents are all called 'uncles' in the West. In China however, the father's elder brothers are called bóbo [伯伯] and his younger brothers are called shúshu [叔叔]. All the mother's brothers are called jiùjiu [舅舅]. Similarly, there are different forms of address for the father's sisters, the mother's sisters and the wives of the uncles—all of whom are called 'aunts' or 'aunties' in the West.

Elder brothers are called gēge [哥哥] and elder sisters are called jiějie [姊姊] by their younger siblings. If there is more than one elder brother or sister, an order title is added ahead of the address, i.e. dàgē [大哥], èrgē [二哥], sāngē [三哥], dàjiě [大姊], èrjiě [二姊], sānjiě [三姊], etc. This also applies to cousins, i.e. elder cousins are called gēge [哥哥] and jiějie [姊姊] by their younger cousins.

Some addresses are not only used among relatives, they are also commonly used among friends or even strangers. People often add the surname of an elder friend ahead of gēge [哥哥] or jiějie [姊姊] to address him/her. For example, they call an elder male friend whose surname is Lín [林] as Lín Gē [林哥], and call an elder female friend whose surname is Lǐ [李] as Lǐ Jiě [李姊]. To children who are strangers, people simply call them xiǎo dìdi [小弟弟] or xiǎo mèimei [小妹妹].

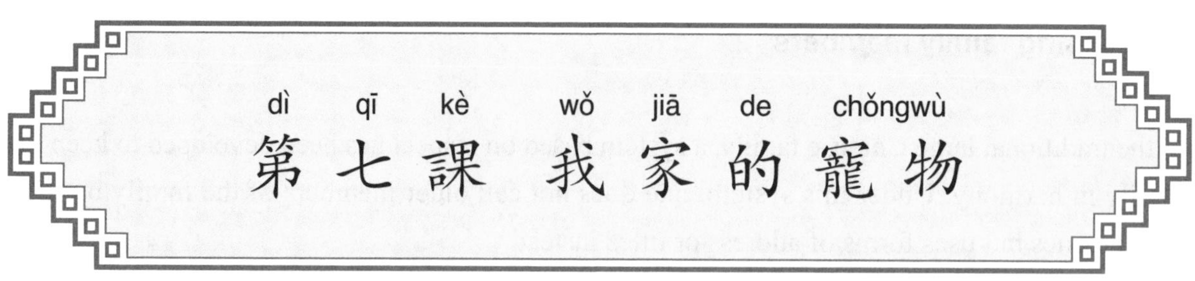

dì qī kè wǒ jiā de chǒngwù
第七課 我家的寵物

1 What pets do you have?

chǒngwù
你家有什麽寵物？

zhī gǒu
我家有兩隻狗。

pī mǎ
我家有四匹馬。

tiáo jīnyú
我家有六條金魚。

zhī māo
我家有五隻貓。

zhī niǎo
我家有三隻鳥。

2 Opposites

pī hěn dà
這匹馬很大。

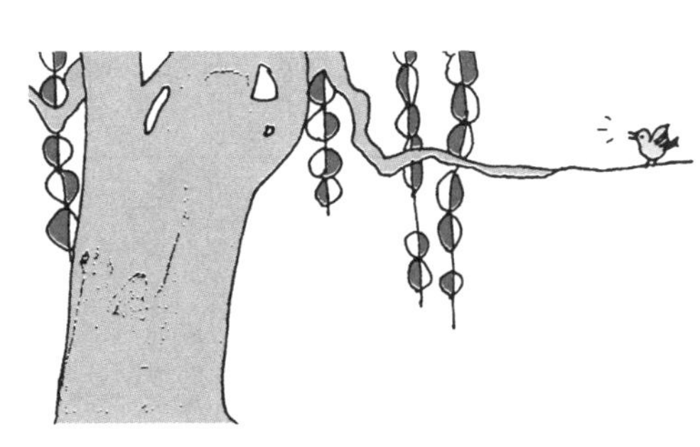

zhī niǎo hěn xiǎo
那隻鳥很小。

hěn xiōng
這隻狗很凶。

māo kě'ài
這隻貓很可愛。

xiōng
這個人很凶。

kě'ài
這個妹妹很可愛。

3 A cute dog

那隻狗是誰的？
是我的。

你的狗真(zhēn)小。
是啊(a)！牠(tā)很可愛(kě'ài)。

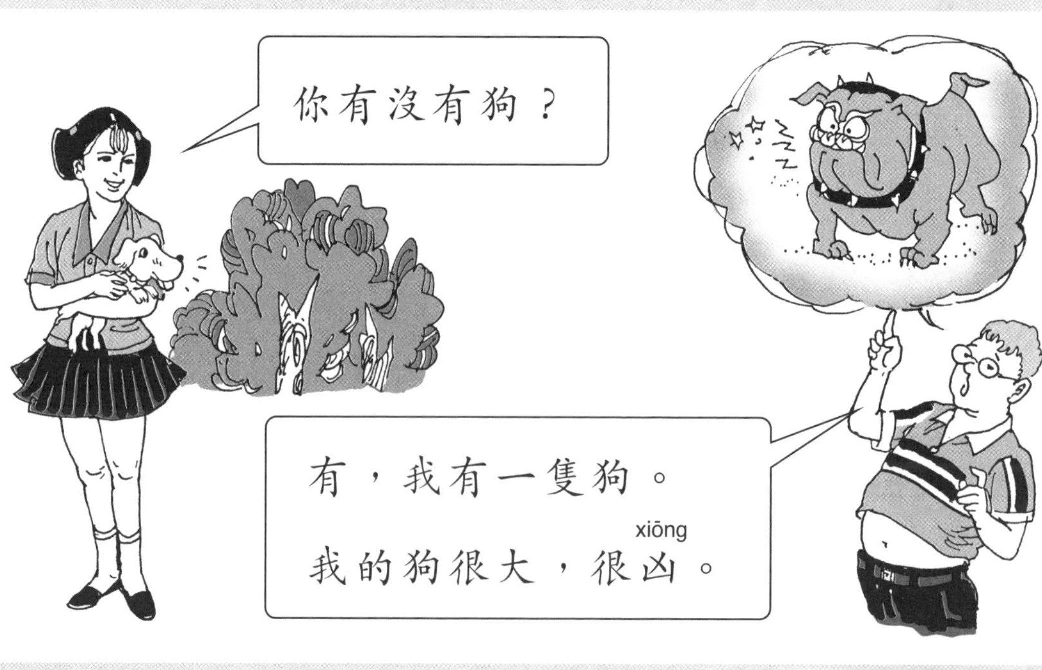
你有沒有狗？
有，我有一隻狗。
我的狗很大，很凶(xiōng)。

Learn the sentences

Stating the number of animals

We learned in lesson six that when stating the number of things, measure words are needed and that the measure word for people is ge 個. When counting birds, dogs or cats, use zhī 隻. The measure word used for horse is pī 匹 and for fish tiáo 條.

zhī gǒu
我家有三隻狗。

pī mǎ
他家有兩匹馬。

tiáo jīnyú
她家有五條金魚。

Asking about pets and family members

To ask What pets do you have? say Nǐ jiā yǒu shéme chǒngwù? 你家有什麼寵物? To answer the question, replace shéme chǒngwù 什麼寵物 with the kind of pet you have. To ask about animals, use dòngwù 動物 instead. The same sentence pattern can be used to ask What family members do you have ? Nǐ jiā yǒu shéme rén? 你家有什麼人?

chǒngwù 你家有什麼寵物? dòngwù 你家有什麼動物?	māo 我家有六隻貓。 pī 我家有四匹馬。 hé māo 我家有一隻狗和兩隻貓。
你家有什麼人?	hé 我家有爸爸、媽媽、哥哥和我。 hé 我家有媽媽、弟弟和我。

Describing things

Measure words are not only used between the number and the object, they are also used with the words zhè 這 and nà 那. To say this dog, say zhè zhī gǒu 這隻狗.

An adjective in Chinese is used in front of the noun it qualifies, therefore to say big dog, say dà gǒu 大狗. When an adjective is used after the noun, it turns into a special kind of verb called a stative verb. Stative verbs take the place of the verb 是 shì, and normally use adverbs such as hěn 很 (very) and zhēn 真 (really) in front of them. To say This dog is very big. say Zhè zhī gǒu hěn dà. 這隻狗很大。 Notice that the verb shì 是 is not needed.

這隻狗很(hěn)大。
這隻貓(māo)很可愛(kě'ài)。
那個人很凶(xiōng)。

Asking if someone has pets

We learned in lessons five and six that the question word ma 嗎 can be placed at the end of a statement to change it into a question. There is another way to change a statement into a question, that is to add a negative form of the verb right after the verb in the statement. There are now two verbs in the sentence: the original verb followed by the negative of the same verb. So to ask Do you have a dog? say:

Nǐ jiā yǒu gǒu <u>ma</u>? 你家有狗<u>嗎</u>?	or	Nǐ jiā yǒu <u>méi yǒu</u> gǒu? 你家有<u>沒有</u>狗?

It is important to become familiar with these two ways of asking questions as they are both commonly used by the Chinese.

你家有狗嗎?	有，我家有一隻狗。 沒有，我家沒有狗。
你家有沒有狗?	有，我家有兩隻狗。 我家沒有狗。

New words and expressions

寵物	chǒngwù	pet chǒng- to spoil, to favor; wù- object, thing
隻	zhī	[a measure word used for some animals, i.e. dogs, cats, birds]
狗	gǒu	dog
匹	pī	[a measure word used for horses, pronounced as pǐ in China]
馬	mǎ	horse
條	tiáo	[a measure word for some long and thin objects]
金魚	jīnyú	goldfish jīn- gold; yú- fish
貓	māo	cat
鳥	niǎo	bird
很	hěn	very
大	dà	big, large
小	xiǎo	small, little (in size)
凶	xiōng	fierce, ferocious
可愛	kě'ài	lovely kě- lovely, can, may; ài- to love
真	zhēn	really
是啊	shì a	yes, yeah (shows agreement)
牠	tā	it (animal) For object, use 它 tā.
動物	dòngwù	animal dòng- to move; wù- object, thing
跑來跑去	pǎolái-pǎoqù	to run around pǎo- to run; lái- to come; qù- to go
牠們	tāmen	they (plural of tā 牠)
都	dōu	all

Something about characters

When describing something big, we often extend our arms to help our description. The early form of the character 大 dà (big) was written as , which has a similar appearance to a person standing with legs apart and arms extended. The early form of the character 小 xiǎo (small) was written as , resembling a picture of a person with his arms at his side to indicate small.

Write the characters

chǒng
to spoil

wù
object, thing

zhī
[measure word]

gǒu
dog

mǎ
horse

很
hěn
very

dà
big

xiǎo
little, small

méi
[negative word]

Supplementary words

Living things around us

熊貓	xióngmāo	panda
袋鼠	dàishǔ	kangaroo
無尾熊	wúwěixióng	koala (called kǎolā 考拉 or shùxióng 樹熊 in China)
蒼蠅	cāngyíng	fly
蚊子	wénzi	mosquito
螞蟻	mǎyǐ	ant
蟑螂	zhāngláng	cockroach
蝴蝶	húdié	butterfly
蜜蜂	mìfēng	bee
鴨子	yāzi	duck
蝙蝠	biǎnfú	bat
鱷魚	èyú	crocodile

我家的寵物

A family portrait

我叫馬九山。我家有四個人。我有爸爸、媽媽和一個妹妹。

我爸爸今年四十七歲。他是老師。我媽媽三十九歲。她是醫生(yīshēng)。我今年十二歲，我妹妹六歲。我們都是學生(xuéshēng)。

我家有很多寵物。我們有三隻貓(māo)，一隻鳥(niǎo)和兩隻狗。貓(māo)是媽媽的，鳥(niǎo)是妹妹的。狗一隻是爸爸的，一隻是我的。爸爸的狗很大，很凶(xiōng)；我的狗很小，很可愛(kě'ài)。

The more the better?

Something to know

老鼠	lǎoshǔ	rat, mouse
牛	niú	cow, ox
老虎	lǎohǔ	tiger
兔子	tùzi	rabbit, hare
龍	lóng	dragon
蛇	shé	snake, serpent
馬	mǎ	horse
羊	yáng	goat, ram
猴子	hóuzi	monkey
雞	jī	rooster, chicken
狗	gǒu	dog
豬	zhū	pig, boar

The twelve animals of the Chinese zodiac

Unlike the Western zodiac, which is a twelve-month cycle, the Chinese zodiac is a twelve-year cycle and is based on twelve animals, called shí'èr shēngxiào [十二生肖]. Each animal represents a year and the corresponding zodiac sign is thought to affect the prosperity of that year and the fate of those born that year.

People born in the year of the 'rat' are presumed to be intelligent and popular; those born in the year of the 'ox' are methodical and conscientious workers. The 'tiger' person is courageous and charismatic; the 'rabbit' is a well-mannered pacifist; the 'dragon' is ambitious and has the quality of leadership; the 'snake' has an active mind and enjoys a challenge; the 'horse' is charming and enjoys being the center of attention; the 'goat' is creative and has an easy-going nature; the 'monkey' is imaginative and curious; the 'rooster' is flamboyant and well-read; the 'dog' is honorable and has a strong sense of fair play; the 'pig' is honest and has an understanding nature.

The rat	The ox	The tiger
1948年2月10日－1949年1月28日	1949年1月29日－1950年2月16日	1950年2月17日－1951年2月 5日
1960年1月28日－1961年2月14日	1961年2月15日－1962年2月 4日	1962年2月 5日－1963年1月24日
1972年2月15日－1973年2月 2日	1973年2月 3日－1974年1月22日	1974年1月23日－1975年2月10日
1984年2月 2日－1985年2月19日	1985年2月20日－1986年2月 8日	1986年2月 9日－1987年1月28日
1996年2月19日－1997年2月 7日	1997年2月 8日－1998年1月27日	1998年1月28日－1999年2月15日

The rabbit	The dragon	The snake
1951年2月 6日－1952年1月26日	1952年1月27日－1953年2月13日	1953年2月14日－1954年2月 2日
1963年1月25日－1964年2月12日	1964年2月13日－1965年2月 1日	1965年2月 2日－1966年1月20日
1975年2月11日－1976年1月30日	1976年1月31日－1977年2月17日	1977年2月18日－1978年2月 6日
1987年1月29日－1988年2月16日	1988年2月17日－1989年2月 5日	1989年2月 6日－1990年1月26日
1999年2月16日－2000年2月 4日	2000年2月 5日－2001年1月23日	2001年1月24日－2002年2月11日

The horse	The goat	The monkey
1954年2月 3日－1955年1月23日	1955年1月24日－1956年2月11日	1956年2月12日－1957年1月30日
1966年1月21日－1967年2月 8日	1967年2月 9日－1968年1月29日	1968年1月30日－1969年2月16日
1978年2月 7日－1979年1月27日	1979年1月28日－1980年2月15日	1980年2月16日－1981年2月 4日
1990年1月27日－1991年2月14日	1991年2月15日－1992年2月 3日	1992年2月 4日－1993年1月22日
2002年2月12日－2003年1月31日	2003年2月 1日－2004年1月21日	2004年1月22日－2005年2月 8日

The rooster	The dog	The pig
1957年1月31日－1958年2月17日	1958年2月18日－1959年2月 7日	1959年2月 8日－1960年1月27日
1969年2月17日－1970年2月 5日	1970年2月 6日－1971年1月26日	1971年1月27日－1972年2月14日
1981年2月 5日－1982年1月24日	1982年1月25日－1983年2月12日	1983年2月13日－1984年2月 1日
1993年1月23日－1994年2月 9日	1994年2月10日－1995年1月30日	1995年1月31日－1996年2月18日

The Chinese zodiac is based on the lunar calendar, so the first day of the Chinese year is not the first of January as on the calendar we use today. The chart above will help you find your Chinese zodiac sign. Most Chinese know the sign of the animal in which they were born and fortune-tellers sometimes take it into consideration when people seek advice in choosing a wife or a husband. However this is regarded as superstitious by some people.

Why these twelve animals?

Long ago, people did not know how to count the years and so they asked the Jade Emperor, Yùhuáng Dàdì [玉皇大帝], for help. The Jade Emperor decided to hold a race through a forest and across a river on his birthday with all of the animals as competitors and decreed that each of the first twelve would have a year named after it.

At the time, the rat and the cat were good friends and so they decided to help each other. Worrying that they might sleep in, they asked the ox, who was an early riser, for help. On the morning of the race, the ox, seeing that the rat and the cat were too sleepy to get up, told them to jump on his back and he would carry them. When the ox was crossing the river, the rat woke up and realized that the cat, who was a fast runner, would certainly come first, so he pushed the cat into the river. As soon as the ox reached the river bank the rat ran as fast as he could and won the race, with the ox in second place. The tiger came third and the rabbit, who jumped across the river on the backs of the other animals, came fourth. The dragon, who was certainly the fastest but had to go to the east to make rain, came fifth. The snake and the horse came next, followed by the goat, the monkey and the rooster, who shared a tree trunk to cross the river. The dog came eleventh and finally the pig managed to make last place.

The cat finally arrived while the twelve victorious animals were celebrating. When he found that he was too late he tried to catch the rat for revenge and that is why cats, to this day, like to catch rats and mice to eat.

The giant panda

The giant panda, called dà xióngmāo [大熊貓], is a unique Chinese animal and its cuddly appearance has made it popular throughout the world. Its diet consists mainly of bamboo. To adapt to this special diet, the panda developed a special sixth digit on its paws to help it grab and hold the young bamboo shoots.

The decrease in the area of bamboo forests has caused the number of pandas to decline. In 1988, it was estimated that the number had dwindled to around 800. The Chinese Government has now established twelve reserves in the provinces of Sichuan [Sìchuān 四川], Gansu [Gānsù 甘肅] and Shaanxi [Shǎnxī 陝西]. The most popular is the Wolong reserve in Sichuan.

There is a legend about why pandas have black fur surrounding their eyes. Once, a shepherd sacrificed his life rescuing a young panda from being eaten by a leopard. The pandas held a ceremony to honor the heroic shepherd and they were so sad during the ceremony that they wept until the tears stained the fur surrounding their eyes, and the stain remains today.

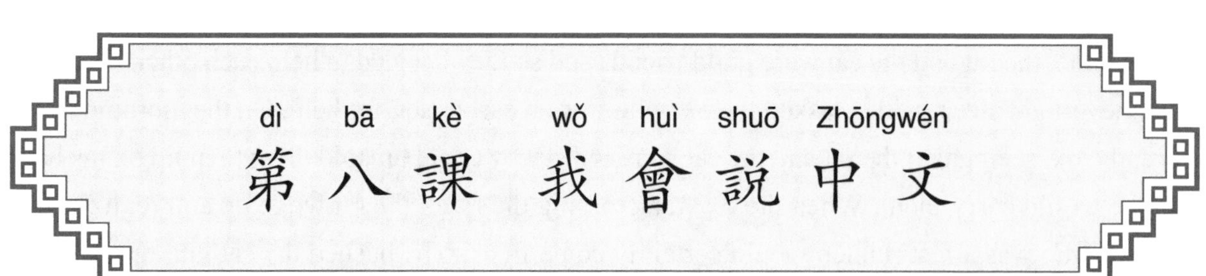

1 Countries

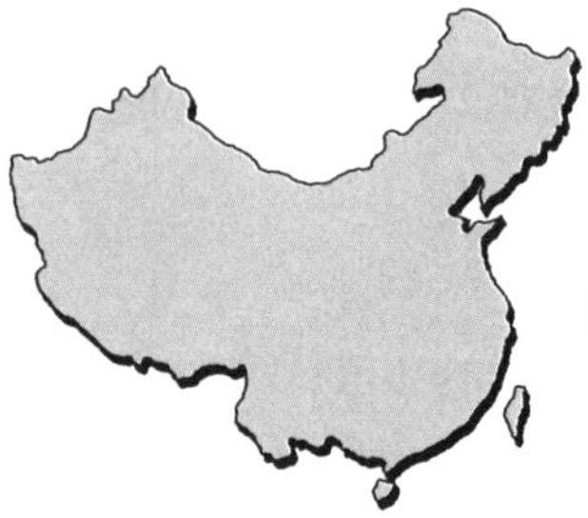

Zhōngguó
中國

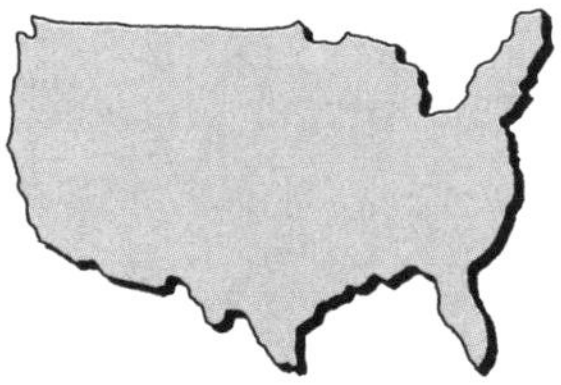

Měiguó
美國

Jiānádà
加拿大

Yīngguó
英國

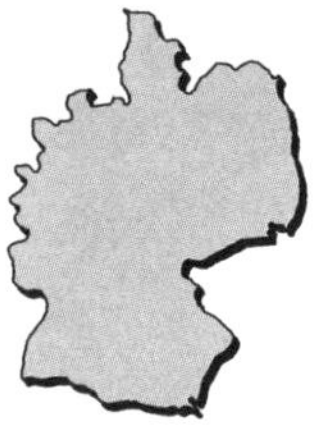

Déguó
德國

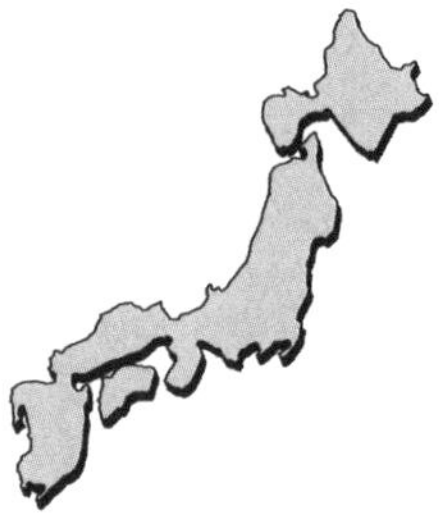

Rìběn
日本

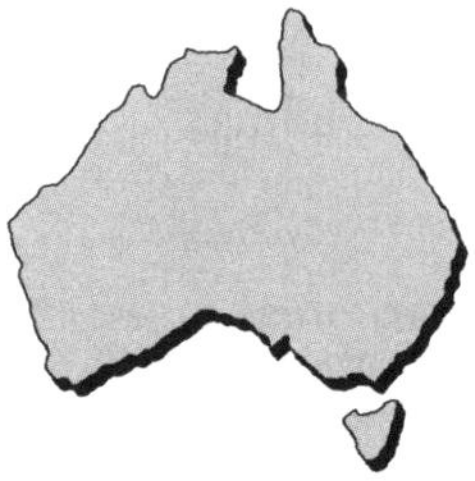

Àozhōu
澳洲

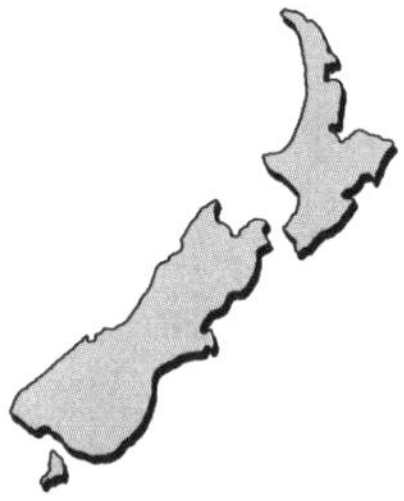

Niǔxīlán
紐西蘭

2 Where are you from?

nǎ

大偉，你是哪國人？

Měiguórén
我是美國人。

nǎ
你是哪國人？

我是中國人。

Mǎkè nǎ
馬克，你是哪國人？

Jiānádàrén
我是加拿大人。

Yīngguórén
我爸爸是英國人。

你媽媽也是英國人嗎？

不是，她是美國人。

3 I am not American

不是。我是加拿大人。

4 Can you speak Chinese?

Learn the sentences

Asking about someone's nationality

To state a person's nationality, simply add rén 人 after the name of the country.

中國	Zhōngguó	>	中國人	Zhōngguórén	Chinese
美國	Měiguó	>	美國人	Měiguórén	American
加拿大	Jiānádà	>	加拿大人	Jiānádàrén	Canadian
英國	Yīngguó	>	英國人	Yīngguórén	British
德國	Déguó	>	德國人	Déguórén	German
日本	Rìběn	>	日本人	Rìběnrén	Japanese
澳洲	Àozhōu	>	澳洲人	Àozhōurén	Australian
紐西蘭	Niǔxīlán	>	紐西蘭人	Niǔxīlánrén	New Zealander

To ask a person his/her nationality, say Nǐ shì nǎ guó rén? 你是哪國人? To answer the question, replace nǎ guó rén 哪國人 with the nationality.

你是哪國人？(nǎ guó)	我是美國人。 我是中國人。
他是哪國人？(nǎ)	他是日本人。(Rìběnrén)
她是哪國人？	她是加拿大人。(Jiānádàrén)

Asking if someone is of a certain nationality

We learned in lesson seven that there are two ways to ask questions that can be answered by saying yes or no; both ways can be used to ask someone if he or she is of a certain nationality. To ask Are you Chinese? say:

Nǐ shì Zhōngguórén ma? 你是中國人嗎?	or	Nǐ shì bú shì Zhōngguórén? 你是不是中國人?

你是中國人嗎？ 他是德國人嗎？ (Déguórén)	是啊(a)，我是中國人。 不是，我不是中國人。 是的，他是德國人(Déguórén)。 他不是德國人。
你是不是中國人？ 他是不是英國人？ (Yīngguórén)	是，我是中國人。 我不是中國人。 他是英國人(Yīngguórén)。 他不是英國人。

Asking about language ability

To ask someone if he or she speaks a certain language, again both ways of asking questions can be used.

Nǐ huì shuō Zhōngwén ma? 你會說中文嗎? or Nǐ huì bú huì shuō Zhōngwén? 你會不會說中文?

你會說中文嗎？(huì shuō Zhōngwén) 他會說英語嗎？(Yīngyǔ)	我會。 我會說一點。(yìdiǎn) 會，他會說英語。(Yīngyǔ) 不會，他不會說英語。(bú)
你會不會說中文？(Zhōngwén) 你會不會說日語？(Rìyǔ) 他會不會說德語？(Déyǔ)	我會說一點。(yìdiǎn) 我不會說日語。(Rìyǔ) 他會。 他不會。

Describing language ability

To say You speak very well. say Nǐ shuō de hěn hǎo. 你說得很好。 To reply Not at all, say Nǎlǐ, nǎlǐ. 哪裡，哪裡。 Chinese use de 得 after a verb to lead to the degree or result of the action of this verb, i.e. to say speak very well, say shuō de hěn hǎo 說得很好, and to say don't speak well, say shuō de bù hǎo 說得不好。

你說得很好。(de) 我說得不好。(de)	哪裡，哪裡。(nǎlǐ) 哪裡，你說得很好。

New words and expressions

會	huì	can, to be able to
說	shuō	to speak, to say
中文	Zhōngwén	Chinese language Zhōng- China, middle; wén- language
中國	Zhōngguó	China zhōng- center, middle; guó- country
美國	Měiguó	America (transliteration), USA měi- beautiful
加拿大	Jiānádà	Canada (transliteration) jiā- to add; ná- to take; dà- big
英國	Yīngguó	England (transliteration) yīng- hero
德國	Déguó	Germany (transliteration- Deutschland) dé- virtue, morals
日本	Rìběn	Japan rì- sun, day; běn- basis, origin
澳洲	Àozhōu	Australia, also called Àodàlìyà 澳大利亞 in China ào- bay; zhōu- continent; dà- big; lì- sharp; yà- Asia, second
紐西蘭	Niǔxīlán	New Zealand, called Xīnxīlán 新西蘭 in China niǔ- bound; xī- west; lán- orchid; xīn- new
哪	nǎ	which
國	guó	country
對不起	duìbùqǐ	excuse me, sorry
沒關係	méi guānxì	it doesn't matter, that's all right méi- not; guānxì- matter
請問	qǐngwèn	may I ask qǐng- please; wèn- to ask
小妹妹	xiǎo mèimei	little girl
不會	bú huì	to be unable to, cannot
咦	yí	why! huh! (indicating surprise)
一點	yìdiǎn	a little, a bit, also said as 一點兒 yìdiǎnr
得	de	(used after a verb to indicate the degree or result)
哪裡	nǎlǐ	not at all (said when praised; literally *where*)
英語	Yīngyǔ	English language
日語	Rìyǔ	Japanese language
德語	Déyǔ	German language

Write the characters

zhōng
middle

guó
country

měi
beautiful

jiā
to add, plus

ná
to take

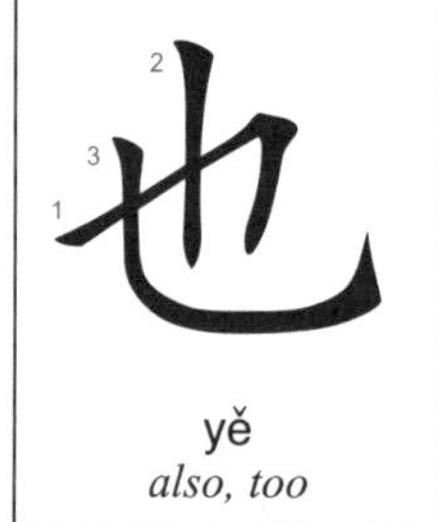

yě
also, too

huì
can, be able to

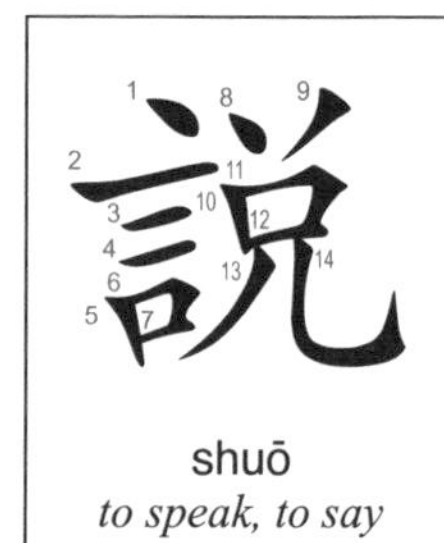

shuō
to speak, to say

A personal profile

她姓(xìng)山口，叫(jiào)小美，今年(jīnnián)十六歲，是學生(xuéshēng)。小美是美國人。她爸爸是日本人(Rìběnrén)，媽媽是中國人。小美有一個哥哥、兩個姊姊和一個妹妹。小美會說英語(Yīngyǔ)、中文(Zhōngwén)和(hé)日語(Rìyǔ)。她英語(Yīngyǔ)和(hé)中文(Zhōngwén)說得(de)很好，日語(Rìyǔ)說得不好。小美的寵物是一匹(pǐ)馬和(hé)一隻鳥(niǎo)。她的馬叫山山；她的鳥叫亞亞。山山很小，很可愛(kě'ài)；亞亞很大，很凶(xiōng)。

Something about characters

An early form of the character 中 zhōng (center or middle) was written as 中, which looks like a vertical line through the center or middle of a mouth. A weapon 戈, a mouth 口, and earth 一 within a boundary 口 forms 國 guó (country), indicating that people use weapons to defend the land of their country.

Supplementary words

Countries

台灣	Táiwān	Taiwan	印度	Yìndù	India
香港	Xiānggǎng	Hong Kong	泰國	Tàiguó	Thailand
法國	Fàguó	France	馬來西亞	Mǎláixīyǎ	Malaysia
愛爾蘭	Ài'ěrlán	Ireland	新加坡	Xīnjiāpō	Singapore
義大利	Yìdàlì	Italy	越南	Yuènán	Vietnam
希臘	Xīlà	Greece	菲律賓	Fēilùbīn	the Philippines
新幾內亞	Xīnjǐnèiyǎ	New Guinea	俄羅斯	Èluósī	Russia
墨西哥	Mòxīgē	Mexico	南非	Nánfēi	South Africa
瑞士	Ruìshì	Switzerland	西班牙	Xībānyá	Spain

The bird's words

tā Zhōngwén
牠會説中文。

tā
牠不會。

tā
牠會。

Zhōngwén Yīngyǔ
牠不會説中文，牠會説英語。

bǐ
牠會説「筆」。

bǐ
那不是「筆」，那是 "bee"。

牠會説「狗」。

那不是「狗」，那是 "go"。

shū
牠會説「你的書」。

shū
那不是「你的書」，那是 "Need a shoe"!

Something to know

'Mandarin' the official Chinese language

'Mandarin' is called different names by the Chinese living in different places. Since the introduction of Pinyin and simplified characters in China, there are also variations in the form of Mandarin being used. You will find that in your local Chinese community, characters used in newspapers, publications and even menus are printed in traditional characters, while publications from China are in simplified form.

Country / area	Terms	Pronunciation system	Style of character
China	Pǔtōnghuà 普通話 Hànyǔ 漢語 Zhōngwén 中文	Pinyin	simplified
Taiwan	Guóyǔ 國語 Zhōngwén 中文	Phonetic symbols (ㄅㄆㄇㄈ…)	traditional
Singapore	Huáyǔ 華語	Pinyin	simplified
Hong Kong	Zhōngwén 中文 Pǔtōnghuà 普通話	Phonetic symbols, changing to Pinyin	traditional, changing to simplified
Overseas Chinese communities	Huáyǔ 華語 Zhōngwén 中文	mainly Phonetic symbols	mainly traditional

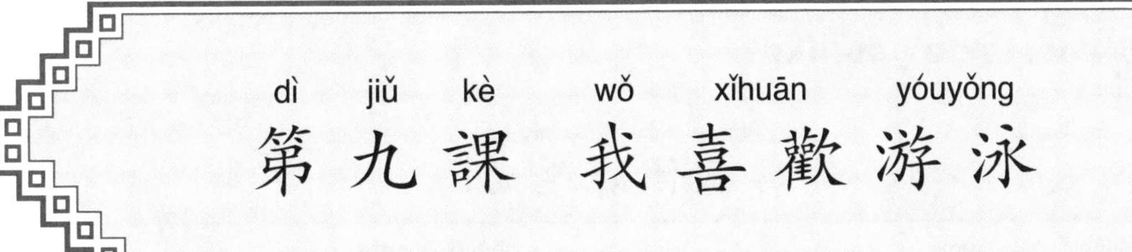

dì jiǔ kè wǒ xǐhuān yóuyǒng

第九課 我喜歡游泳

1 Sports

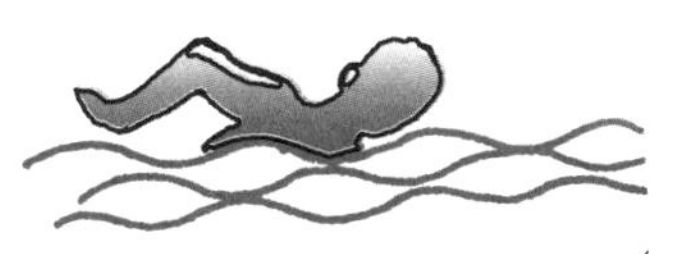

yóuyǒng
游泳

qíchē
騎車

pǎobù
跑步

tī zúqiú
踢足球

dǎ lánqiú
打籃球

dǎ wǎngqiú
打網球

pīngpāngqiú
打乒乓球

bàngqiú
打棒球

2 What sports do you like?

xǐhuān yùndòng
你喜歡什麼運動?

xǐhuān tī zúqiú
我喜歡踢足球。

xǐhuān qíchē
我喜歡騎車。

wǎngqiú
我喜歡打網球。

pǎobù
我喜歡跑步。

Dàwěi yóuyǒng
大偉，你喜歡游泳嗎？

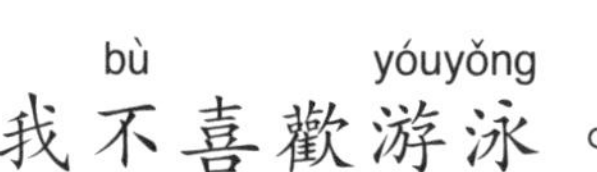

ne
我喜歡，你呢？

bù yóuyǒng
我不喜歡游泳。

lánqiú
我喜歡打籃球。
你喜歡打籃球嗎？

我不喜歡。

3 Let's play baseball

wèi　qù　bàngqiú
喂，我們去打棒球，好嗎？

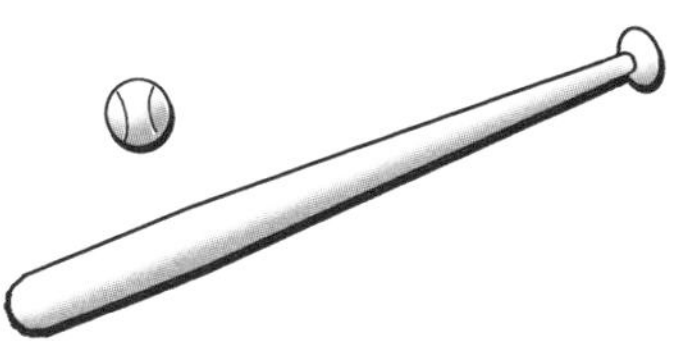

a　zuì　bàngqiú
好啊！我最喜歡打棒球。

bú qù　zuì
我不去。我最不喜歡打棒球。

zǒu ba
我們走吧！
zàijiàn　Lánlán
再見，蘭蘭！

再見！

Mǎkè　pīngpāngqiú
馬克，我們去打乒乓球，好嗎？

duìbùqǐ　máng
對不起，我不去。我很忙。

Learn the sentences

Asking what sports someone likes

To ask What sports do you like? say Nǐ xǐhuān shéme yùndòng? 你喜歡什麼運動？ To answer the question, replace shéme yùndòng 什麼運動 with the name of the sport.

你喜歡(xǐhuān)什麼運動(yùndòng)？	我喜歡游泳(yóuyǒng)。
	我喜歡打網球(wǎngqiú)。
	我喜歡騎車(qíchē)。
	我喜歡踢(tī)足球(zúqiú)。
他喜歡什麼運動？	他喜歡跑步(pǎobù)。
	他喜歡打棒球(bàngqiú)。
	他喜歡踢足球。
她喜歡什麼運動？	她喜歡打乒乓球(pīngpāngqiú)。
	她喜歡打籃球(lánqiú)。

Asking if someone likes a certain sport

To ask someone whether he/she likes a particular sport, say:

Nǐ xǐhuān... ma? 你喜歡……嗎?	or	Nǐ xǐhuān bù xǐhuān...? 你喜歡不喜歡……?

The expression xǐhuān bù xǐhuān 喜歡不喜歡 can be shortened to xǐ bù xǐhuān 喜不喜歡

你喜歡打籃球(lánqiú)嗎？ 你喜歡打乒乓球(pīngpāngqiú)嗎？ 你喜不喜歡踢(tī)足球(zúqiú)？ 你喜不喜歡騎車(qíchē)？	我喜歡。 我不喜歡。
他喜歡打棒球(bàngqiú)嗎？ 他喜不喜歡游泳(yóuyǒng)？	他喜歡。 他不喜歡。

Suggesting an activity

English uses the expression Let's... to suggest an activity. In Chinese, say Wǒmen qù..., hǎo ma? 我們去……，好嗎? To answer OK. say Hǎo a! 好啊！ The a 啊 is used to stress that you think it's a good idea. To answer I'm not going. say Wǒ bú qù. 我不去。

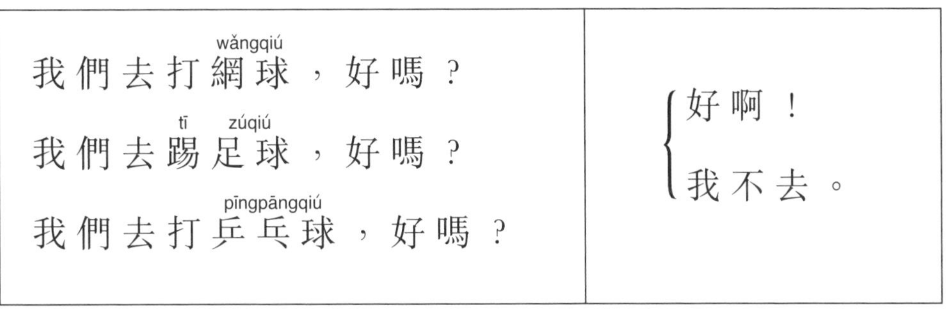

我們去打網球(wǎngqiú)，好嗎？ 我們去踢(tī)足球(zúqiú)，好嗎？ 我們去打乒乓球(pīngpāngqiú)，好嗎？	好啊！ 我不去。

New words and expressions

喜歡	xǐhuān	to like　xǐ- to like, happy; huān- happy
游泳	yóuyǒng	swimming, to swim　yóu- to swim; yǒng- to swim
騎車	qíchē	1. cycling (qí zìyóuchē 騎自由車); 2. to ride a bicycle (qí zìxíngchē 騎自行車 or qí jiǎotàchē 騎腳踏車) qí- to ride on something; chē- vehicle; zìyóu- freedom, free; jiǎo- foot; tà- to tread
跑步	pǎobù	running, to jog　pǎo- to run; bù- step, pace
踢	tī	to kick, to play (soccer)
足球	zúqiú	soccer　zú- foot; qiú- ball
打	dǎ	to hit, to play (tennis, basketball, table tennis etc.)
籃球	lánqiú	basketball　lán- basket; qiú- ball
網球	wǎngqiú	tennis　wǎng- net; qiú- ball
乒乓球	pīngpāngqiú	table tennis　pīng, pāng- sound of the ball hitting the table
棒球	bàngqiú	baseball　bàng- bat; qiú- ball
運動	yùndòng	sports, exercise　yùn- to transport; dòng- to move
喂	wèi	hey!
去	qù	to go
好嗎	hǎo ma	OK? (an expression to ask for agreement)
好啊	hǎo a	good! (agreeing)
最	zuì	most
不去	bú qù	not going [negative form of qù 去]
走	zǒu	to go, to walk
吧	ba	(expression used at the end of a sentence to indicate suggestion)
我們走吧	wǒmen zǒu ba	let's go
忙	máng	busy

Something about characters

When we are happy, we may feel like singing. The character 喜 xǐ (happy) was once written as 喜 which shows music 壴 coming out of a mouth ㅂ. The music is represented by the shape of a drum 豆 with decoration 㞢.

Write the characters

xǐ
to like, happy

huān
happy

yùn
to transport, luck

dòng
to move

dǎ
to hit

qiú
ball

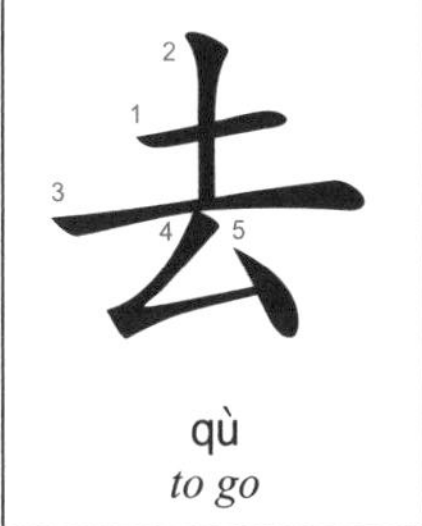

qù
to go

ba
(grammatical word)

Amazing pets

jiào Lín jīnnián
他叫林大利，今年九十四歲，是美國人。他爸爸是中

Lín Zhōngwén yìdiǎn Rìyǔ pǐ
國人。林大利會說中文，也會說一點日語。他有三匹馬、

māo tiáo jīnyú hé niǎo tī zúqiú
四隻狗、兩隻貓、十八條金魚和一隻鳥。他的馬會踢足球；

lánqiú māo yóuyǒng jīnyú
他的狗會打籃球。他的貓喜歡游泳；他的金魚不喜歡貓。

niǎo Yīngyǔ hé Zhōngwén tā zuì xièxie
他的鳥會說英語和中文，牠最喜歡說"謝謝！"

Supplementary words

More Sports

橄欖球	gǎnlǎnqiú	rugby
板球	bǎnqiú	cricket
壘球	lěiqiú	softball
體操	tǐcāo	gymnastics
跳遠	tiàoyuǎn	long jump
跳高	tiàogāo	high jump
田徑	tiánjìng	track and field
保齡球	bǎolíngqiú	bowling (tenpin)
高爾夫球	gāo'ěrfūqiú	golf
排球	páiqiú	volleyball
羽毛球	yǔmáoqiú	badminton
曲棍球	qūgùnqiú	hockey

Something to know

Taijiquan

Tàijíquán [太極拳] (taichi), characterized by its graceful and slow movements, is a traditional Chinese sport and an exercise for the mind as well as the body.

To practice tàijíquán [太極拳], one needs to be relaxed and concentrate on breathing and the flow of each movement. The exercise develops physical endurance, relaxation and mental calm. It is performed by millions of Chinese daily, mainly early in the morning, in parks or anywhere else where there is enough space.

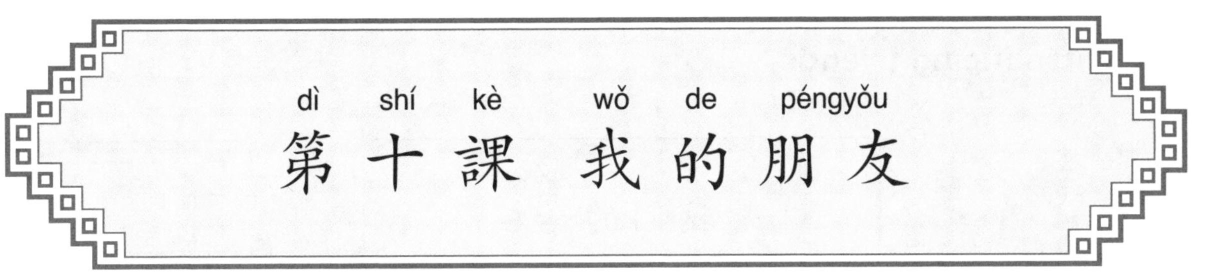

dì shí kè wǒ de péngyǒu
第十課 我的朋友

1 Lanlan's friend

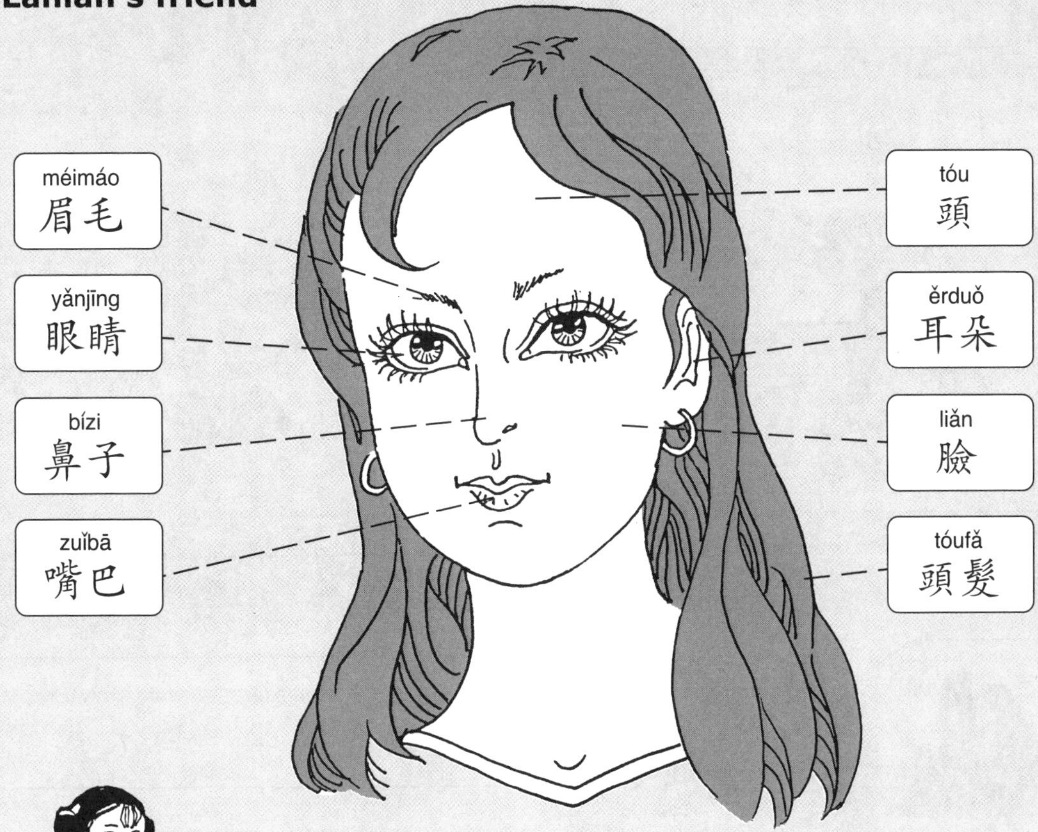

這是我的朋友(péngyǒu)。她叫(jiào)王(Wáng)美怡(Měiyí)。

她今年十四歲，上(shàng)九年級(niánjí)。

她的眼睛(yǎnjīng)很大，嘴巴(zuǐbā)很小；

她的頭髮(tóufǎ)很長，眉毛(méimáo)很短。

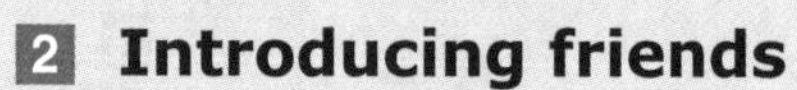

2 Introducing friends

xuéxiào
這是我們的學校。

xuéxiào zhēn
你們的學校真大。

Lánlán
你好，蘭蘭！

你好！

他是誰？

tóngxué Bái Dàwěi
他是我的同學，白大偉。

Dàwěi
大偉，這是我的朋友。她叫
Wáng Měiyí
王美怡。

你好。
Bái Dàwěi
我叫白大偉。

你好。

3 What grade are you in?

Wáng Měiyí shàng niánjí
王美怡，你上幾年級？

ne
我上九年級，你呢？

我上七年級。
Lánlán
蘭蘭也上七年級。

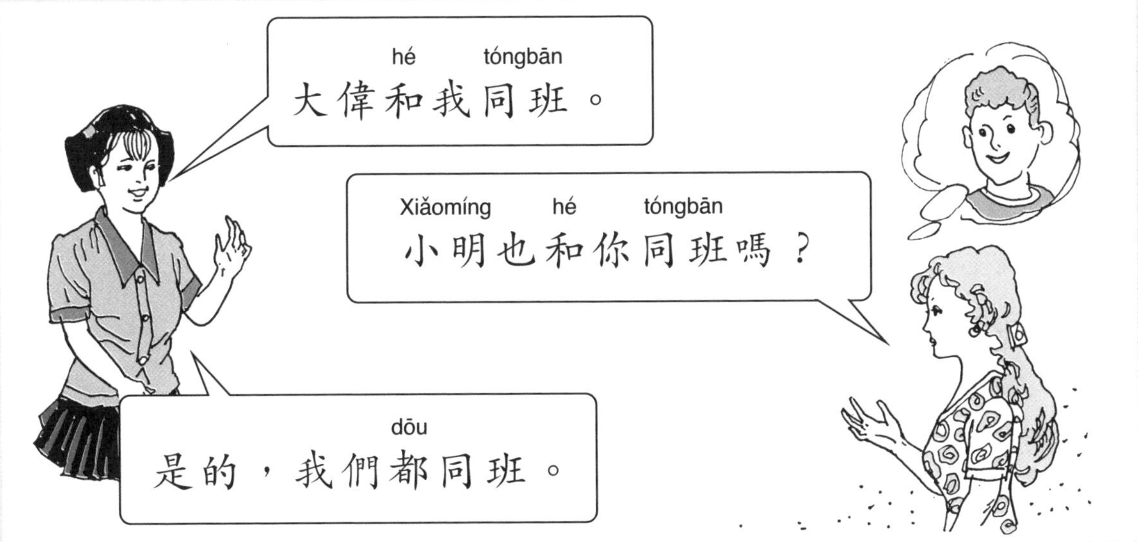

hé tóngbān
大偉和我同班。

Xiǎomíng hé tóngbān
小明也和你同班嗎？

dōu
是的，我們都同班。

Learn the sentences

Asking what grade someone is in at school

To ask What grade are you in? say Nǐ shàng jǐ niánjí? 你上幾年級? To answer, replace the question word jǐ 幾 with the grade.

你上幾年級？ (shàng, niánjí)	我上六年級。 我上七年級。
他上幾年級？	他上五年級。 他上九年級。
她上幾年級？	她上八年級。 她上四年級。

Asking about someone's identity

We learned in lesson four that Tā shì shéi? 他是誰? is used to ask who a person is, and that the answer is the person's name or title. Now we'll learn to answer the question by stating the person's relationship to you or to someone else.

他是誰？	他是我的朋友。 (péngyǒu) 他是我的弟弟。
她是誰？	她是我姊姊的朋友。 她是我媽媽。

Asking if someone is in the same class

To ask Is he in the same class as you? say Tā hé nǐ tóngbān ma? 他和你同班嗎? To answer yes, say shìde 是的; to answer no, say bù 不.

他和你同班嗎？ (hé, tóngbān)	是的，他和我同班。 (tóngbān) 不，他不和我同班。
你和我妹妹同班嗎？	是的，我和她同班。 不，我不和她同班。
你和大偉同班嗎？ (Dàwěi)	是的，我們同班。 不，我們不同班。

A rhyme

cháng méi duǎn tóufǎ yǎn zuǐbā
長眉短頭髮，小眼大嘴巴；

xiàohāhā shuōhuà xiōngbābā
打球笑哈哈，說話凶巴巴。

New words and expressions

朋友	péngyǒu	friend, also said as péngyou　péng- friend; yǒu- friend
眉毛	méimáo	eyebrow, also said as méimao　méi- eyebrow, máo- hair
眼睛	yǎnjīng	eye, also said as yǎnjing　yǎn, jīng- eye
鼻子	bízi	nose
嘴巴	zuǐbā	mouth, also said as zuǐba
頭	tóu	head
耳朵	ěrduǒ	ear, also said as ěrduo　ěr- ear; duǒ- measure word for flower
臉	liǎn	face
頭髮	tóufǎ	hair (on human head), also said as tóufa　tóu- head; fǎ- hair
王	Wáng	a family name　wáng- king
美怡	Měiyí	a given name　měi- beautiful; yí- happy
上	shàng	to go, to attend
年級	niánjí	grade　nián- year; jí- level
長	cháng	long
短	duǎn	short
學校	xuéxiào	school　xué- to learn, to study; xiào- school
同班	tóngbān	same class　tóng- same; bān- class
笑哈哈	xiàohāhā	to laugh heartily, laughingly　xiào- to smile, to laugh
凶巴巴	xiōngbābā	fiercely, ferociously　xiōng- fierce, ferocious

Write the characters

péng
friend

yǒu
friend

jiào
to be called, to call

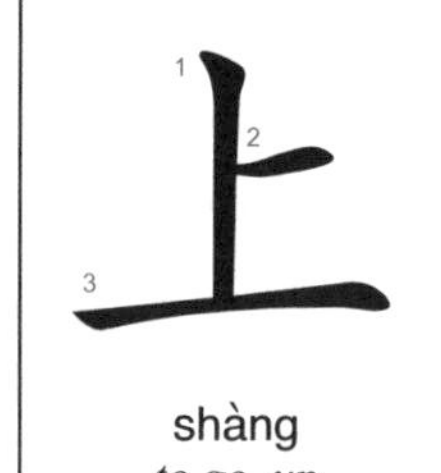
shàng
to go, up

年
nián
year

jí
grade, step

hé, hàn
and

tóng
together, the same

xué
to study

My alien friends

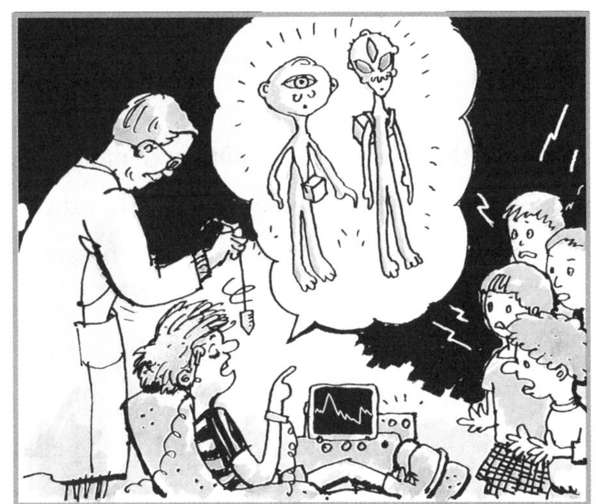

他叫大中，是我的朋友。大中沒有頭髮(tóufǎ)，也沒有眉毛(méimáo)。他有一隻眼睛(yǎnjīng)，兩個鼻子(bízi)，三個耳朵(ěrduǒ)。他的眼睛(yǎnjīng)很大，鼻子(bízi)和嘴巴(zuǐbā)都(dōu)很小。

大中沒有爸爸，也沒有媽媽。他今年五歲，上九年級。大中和小國同班(tóngbān)。小國今年(jīnnián)八歲，上四年級。他有三隻眼睛(yǎnjīng)、四個鼻子(bízi)、五個耳朵(ěrduǒ)……。

Something about characters

The modern form of 朋 péng looks like two moons. An early form of 友 yǒu was written as 㕛, which resembles holding hands. Both of these characters explain the foundation of friendship and are written together to mean friend.

An early form of 上 shàng was written as 丄, which represents an object standing high above the ground.

Something to know

Schools

In China, the school year begins in September with the first semester ending in mid-January. The second semester begins in February (after three weeks' vacation for the Spring Festival—Chinese New Year) and ends in mid-July, leaving six weeks for the summer vacation.

The structure of the regular education system follows a 6–3–3–4 pattern: six years of primary school [xiǎoxué 小學], three years of junior high school [chūzhōng 初中], three years of senior high school [gāozhōng 高中] and four years of college/university education [dàxué 大學]. Entrance examinations to each higher level are very competitive. Keypoint schools, [zhòngdiǎn xuéxiào 重點學校], which are better equipped and have a higher academic standard, are the most popular schools.

In Taiwan, the school year starts in autumn and ends in summer the next year. There are two vacations: winter vacation [hánjià 寒假], around the time of the lunar New Year (end of January to beginning of February) and summer vacation [shǔjià 暑假], from July to late August. The general school system also follows a 6–3–3–4 pattern. Entrance examinations to senior high schools and to universities are also extremely competitive. Public schools are generally more popular than private schools, although there are also some very popular private schools. The National Taiwan University [Táiwān Dàxué 台灣大學] is the most sought after of the universities.

Chinese students have many responsibilities at school. They are responsible for cleaning the classroom and maintaining discipline during class. Every day, students take turns to clean the school grounds in the morning, and to clean their classrooms after school. There is no detention system but students are generally well-behaved. Assembly is held every morning and students exercise in the assembly grounds before going to class or during recess. In some schools in China, an eye exercise, accompanied by music, is practiced during recess.

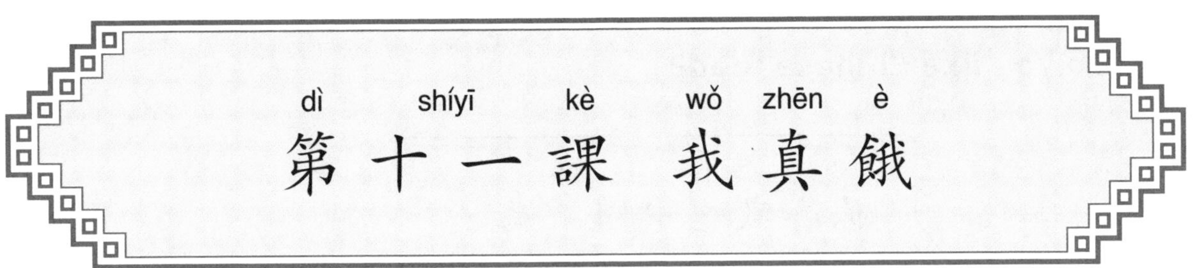

dì shíyī kè wǒ zhēn è

第十一課 我真餓

1 I am hungry

zhēn è
我真餓。

chī diǎn dōngxī
我們去吃點東西吧！

xiǎng chī
你想吃什麼？

xiǎng chī sānmíngzhì
我想吃三明治，

你呢？

è kě
我不餓；我很渴。

hē guǒzhī
我想喝果汁。

hànbǎo
漢堡

bīngqílín
冰淇淋

règǒu
熱狗

niúnǎi
牛奶

2 Do you like Chinese food?

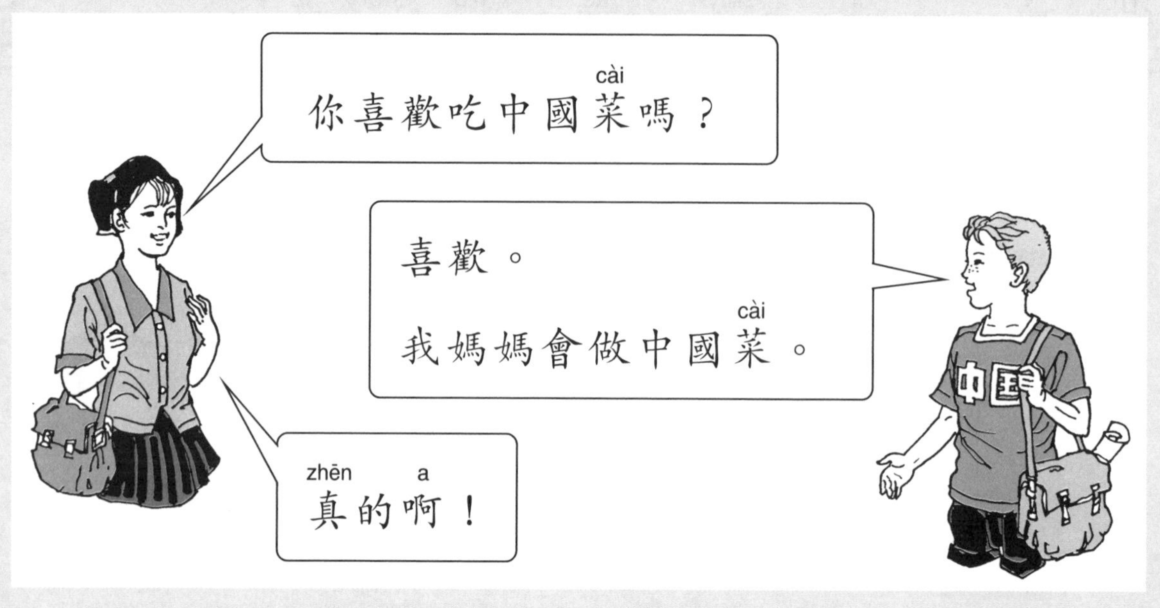

quánjiā dōu
我們全家都喜歡吃中國菜。

gūlǎoròu
我爸爸喜歡吃咕咾肉。

níngméng - jīpiàn
我媽媽喜歡吃檸檬雞片。

chūnjuǎn
我哥哥喜歡春捲。

chǎofàn
我妹妹喜歡炒飯。

zháxiāpiàn
我最喜歡炸蝦片。

3 Can you use chopsticks?

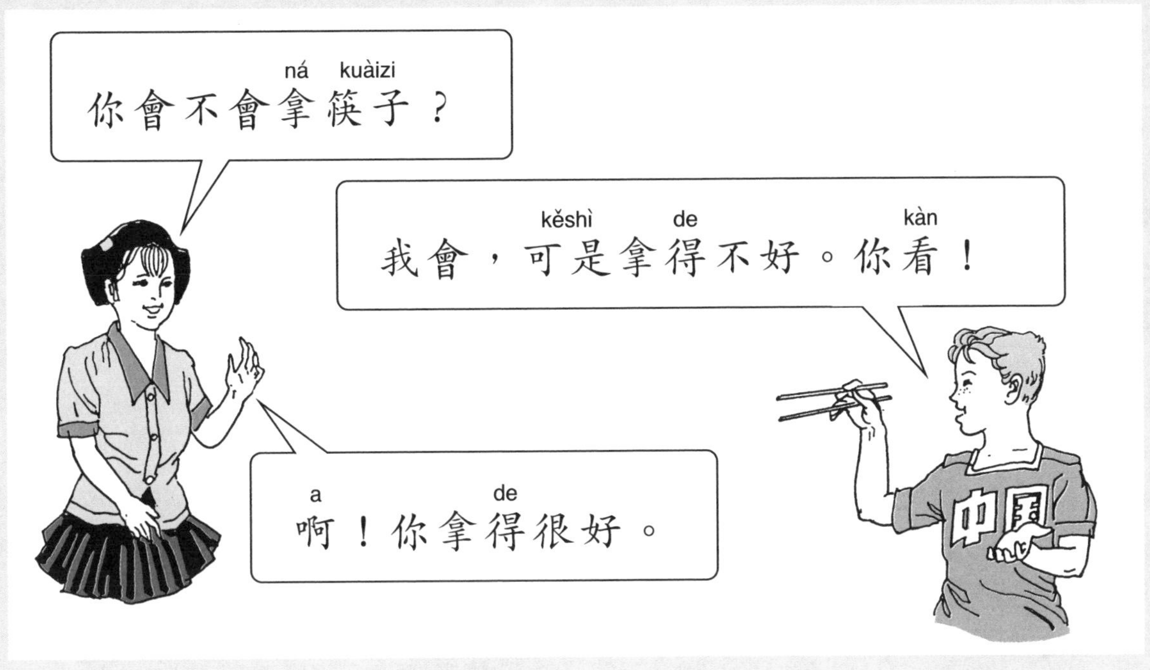

Learn the sentences

Expressing hunger or thirst

We learned about stative verbs in lesson eight. The adjectives è 餓 and kě 渴 can also be used as stative verbs. Remember that when adjectives are used as stative verbs, you may add words such as hěn 很 (very), zhēn 真 (really) or, to make it negative, use bù 不 before the stative verb.

我真餓。(zhēn è)	我不餓。(bú)
我真渴。(kě)	我不渴。(bù)
他很餓。	他不餓。

Asking what someone would like to eat or drink

To ask What would you like to eat/drink? say Nǐ xiǎng chī/hē shéme? 你想吃 / 喝什麼? To answer the question, replace the question word shéme 什麼 with the food/drink you would like to have.

你想吃什麼？(xiǎng)	我想吃漢堡。(hànbǎo) 我想吃冰淇淋。(bīngqílín)
他想吃什麼？	他想吃炒飯。(chǎofàn) 他想吃炸蝦片。(zháxiāpiàn)
你想喝什麼？(hē)	我想喝果汁。(guǒzhī) 我想喝牛奶。(niúnǎi)

Talking about someone's abilities

We learned in lesson eight that to ask Can you speak Chinese? you say Nǐ huì bú huì shuō Zhōngwén? 你會不會說中文? Now the same sentence pattern will be used to ask about other things that people are able to do.

你會不會說中文(Zhōngwén)? 你會不會拿筷子(kuàizi)? 你會不會做(zuò)中國菜? 你會不會游泳(yóuyǒng)? 你會不會踢(tī)足球(zúqiú)?	我會。 我不會。
他會不會說英語(Yīngyǔ)? 他會不會騎車(qíchē)? 他會不會打棒球(bàngqiú)?	他會。 他不會。

New words and expressions

餓	è	hungry
吃	chī	to eat
點	diǎn	a little, a bit (short form of yìdiǎn 一點)
東西	dōngxī	thing, also said as dōngxi dōng- east; xī- west
想	xiǎng	to feel like, to think
三明治	sānmíngzhì	sandwich
渴	kě	thirsty

喝	hē	to drink
果汁	guǒzhī	juice　guǒ- fruit; zhī- juice
漢堡	hànbǎo	hamburger (used in Taiwan), called hànbǎobāo 漢堡包 in China
冰淇淋	bīngqílín	ice cream
熱狗	règǒu	hotdog　rè- hot; gǒu - dog
牛奶	niúnǎi	milk　niú- cow; nǎi- milk
菜	cài	(meal) dish, vegetable
做	zuò	to make, to cook, to do
真的啊！	zhēn de a!	really!
全家	quánjiā	whole family　quán- whole, all; jiā- family
咕咾肉	gūlǎoròu	sweet and sour pork, a Cantonese dish, also called gūlūròu 咕嚕肉
檸檬雞片	níngméng-jīpiàn	lemon chicken　níngméng- lemon; jī- chicken; piàn- thin piece
春捲	chūnjuǎn	spring rolls　chūn- spring; juǎn- roll
炒飯	chǎofàn	fried rice　chǎo- to stir-fry; fàn- cooked rice
炸蝦片	zháxiāpiàn	prawn crackers　zhá- to deep-fry; xiā- prawn; piàn- thin piece
拿	ná	to hold, to take
筷子	kuàizi	chopsticks
可是	kěshì	but
看	kàn	to look, to see
到	dào	to go to, to arrive
吃飯	chī fàn	to have a meal　chī- to eat; fàn- meal, cooked rice
太好了	tài hǎo le	that's great!　tài- too; hǎo- good; le- [stressing the situation]
別客氣	bié kèqì	not at all, you're welcome　bié- don't; kèqì- polite

Write the characters

zhēn
really

è
hungry

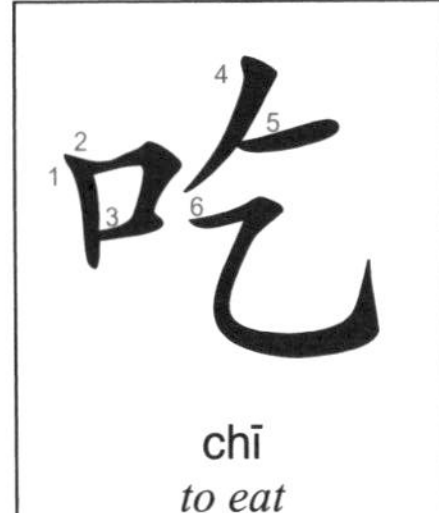

chī
to eat

xiǎng
to think

kě
thirsty

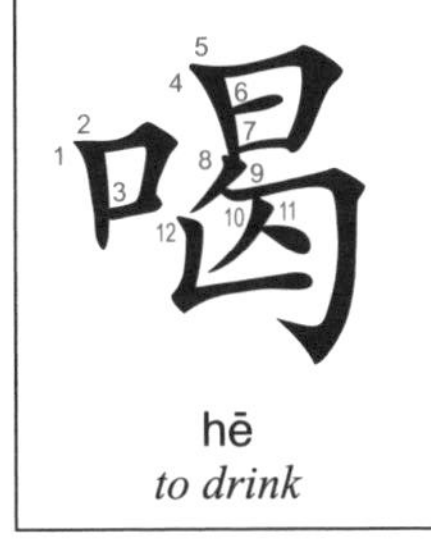

hē
to drink

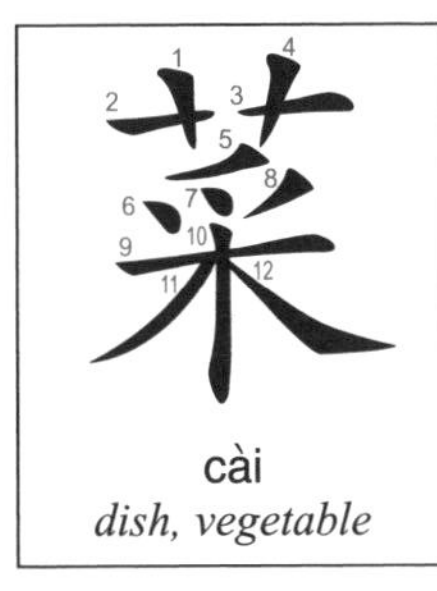

cài
dish, vegetable

fàn
meal, cooked rice

Supplementary words

More food

汽水	qìshuǐ	soda pop
水	shuǐ	water
開水	kāishuǐ	boiled water, drinking water
可樂	kělè	cola
麵包	miànbāo	bread
薯條	shǔtiáo	French fries
奶油	nǎiyóu	butter, also called huángyóu 黄油
餅乾	bǐnggān	cookies
蛋糕	dàngāo	cake
麵	miàn	noodles
湯	tāng	soup
乳酪	rǔlào, rǔluò	cheese
巧克力	qiǎokèlì	chocolate

A midsummer's nightmare
yóuyǒng
我不喜歡游泳！
①

yóuyǒng
我真不喜歡游泳！
②

guǒzhī niúnǎi
我真渴！我想喝果汁，也想喝牛奶。
sānmíngzhì règǒu
我很餓！我想吃三明治，也想吃熱狗。
a chǎofàn chūnjuǎn gūlǎoròu
啊！我想吃媽媽的炒飯、春捲和咕咾肉。
③

yú
我不想吃魚。
我想吃……
Pooh!
④

%@&$!!....
⑤

niǎo
我不喜歡打鳥。
pīngpāngqiú wǎngqiú
我喜歡打乒乓球，喜歡打網球，
lánqiú
喜歡打籃球，……
⑥

我喜歡打…
⑦

BANG!!!
%@&$!!

……這是什麼球？
?

Something to know

Chinese food

The three principles of Chinese food preparation are that the food should look good, smell good and taste good. Food is regarded as good if these three principles are satisfied. As China is vast, there is a great variety of foods and cooking methods. The Beijing style of cooking has lovely snacks, Sichuan cooking is well-known for its hot and spicy flavors, and Guangdong (Cantonese) cooking is famous for its sweet and sour style.

Seasonings and utensils

Despite the great variety in Chinese cooking, the most common seasonings are shallots, ginger, garlic and soy sauce.

Although many tools are used in cooking, the most unique Chinese cooking utensil is the wok [guōzi 鍋子]. The wok serves many functions such as stir-frying, shallow-frying, deep-frying, steaming, and boiling.

On the table, apart from plates and soup bowls, chopsticks [kuàizi 筷子] and rice bowls [wǎn 碗] are essential items. Knives are considered unsuitable to be placed on the dinner table.

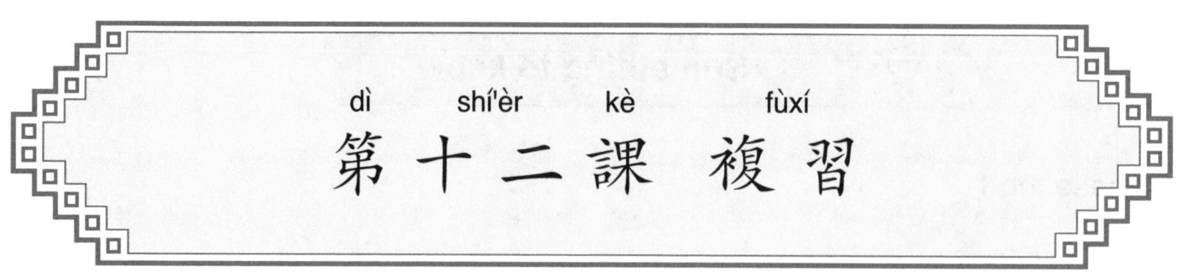

dì shí'èr kè fùxí
第十二課 複習

1 Letter to a friend

Guómíng
國明：

xìng Bái　Bái Dàwěi　yìdiǎn
你好。我姓白，叫白大偉。我是美國人，會說一點

Zhōngwén　xuéshēng　jīnnián
中文。我是學生，今年十二歲，上七年級。我家有

五個人。我有爸爸、媽媽、一個哥哥和一個妹妹。

yīshēng　hùshì　dōu　xuéshēng
我爸爸是醫生，媽媽是護士，哥哥和妹妹都是學生。

tā　kě'ài
我家有一隻狗。牠很小、很可愛。

quánjiā　dōu　zuò
我們全家都喜歡吃中國菜。我媽媽會做中國菜。

zuì　chūnjuǎn　Lǐ　Lánlán
我最喜歡吃春捲。我有一個中國朋友，她叫李蘭蘭。

Lánlán　tóngbān　kuàizi　ná　de
蘭蘭和我同班，她說我筷子拿得很好。

xuéxiào　bàngqiú　yóuyǒng
我們的學校很大。我喜歡打棒球，也喜歡游泳。

你喜歡什麼運動？

zhù
祝你

kuàilè
快樂

大偉

2 Being polite

Expressing thanks	➪	Responding
xièxie 謝謝。		kèqì 不客氣。
xièxie 謝謝你。		bié 別客氣。

Expressing welcome	➪	Responding
huānyíng 歡迎，歡迎。		謝謝。
qǐng jìn 請進。		

Apologizing	➪	Responding
duìbùqǐ 對不起。		guānxì 沒關係。

Praising people	➪	Responding
de 你說得很好。		nǎlǐ 哪裡！
ná 你拿得很好。		哪裡！哪裡！
zuò 你做得很好。		

Asking for help

qǐngwèn
請問，……？

3 Reading signs

Appendix

WORDS AND EXPRESSIONS
Chinese-English

	Traditional	Pinyin	English	Simplified	Lesson
A	阿姨	āyí	mother's sister	阿姨	6
	啊	a	[an exclamation]	啊	4
	愛爾蘭	Ài'ěrlán	Ireland	爱尔兰	8
	澳大利亞	Àodàlìyà	Australia (used in China)	澳大利亚	8
	澳洲	Àozhōu	Australia (used in Taiwan)	澳洲	8
B	八	bā	eight	八	3
	把手放下	bǎ shǒu fàng xià	put down (your) hand	把手放下	2
	把書打開	bǎ shū dǎ kāi	open (your) book	把书打开	2
	爸爸	bàba	dad, father	爸爸	6
	吧	ba	[indicating suggestion]	吧	9
	白	Bái	a family name; bái- white	白	2
	百	bǎi	hundred	百	3
	板球	bǎnqiú	cricket	板球	9
	棒球	bàngqiú	baseball	棒球	9
	保齡球	bǎolíngqiú	bowling (tenpin)	保龄球	9
	保羅	Bǎoluó	Paul	保罗	6
	鼻子	bízi	nose	鼻子	10
	筆	bǐ	pen	笔	5
	蝙蝠	biǎnfú	bat	蝙蝠	7
	別客氣	bié kèqì	you're welcome, not at all	别客气	11
	冰淇淋	bīngqílín	ice cream	冰淇淋	11
	餅乾	bǐnggān	cookies	饼干	11
	伯伯	bóbo	father's elder brother	伯伯	6
	不會	bú huì	unable to, cannot	不会	8
	不客氣	bú kèqì	you're welcome, not at all	不客气	5
	不去	bú qù	not going	不去	9
	不是	bú shì	no (negative form of shì 是)	不是	5
	不要說話	bú yào shuōhuà	do not talk	不要说话	2
	不	bù	no, not (used to negate)	不	5
C	彩色筆	cǎisèbǐ	color pencil	彩色笔	5
	菜	cài	meal, dish, vegetable	菜	11
	蒼蠅	cāngyíng	fly (*n.*)	苍蝇	7
	長	cháng	long	长	10
	炒飯	chǎofàn	fried rice	炒饭	11
	乘以	chéng yǐ	multiplied by	乘以	3

	Traditional	Pinyin	English	Simplified	Lesson
	吃	chī	to eat	吃	11
	吃飯	chī fàn	to have a meal	吃饭	11
	尺	chǐ	ruler	尺	5
	寵物	chǒngwù	pet	宠物	7
	除以	chú yǐ	divided by	除以	3
	窗户	chuānghù	window	窗户	5
	春捲	chūnjuǎn	spring rolls	春卷	11
D	打	dǎ	to hit, to play (basketball, tennis...etc.)	打	9
	大	dà	big, large	大	7
	大概	dàgài	probably	大概	5
	大聲一點	dà shēng yìdiǎn	a little louder	大声一点	2
	大偉	Dàwěi	David	大伟	2
	大熊貓	dà xióngmāo	giant panda	大熊猫	7
	袋鼠	dàishǔ	kangaroo	袋鼠	7
	蛋糕	dàngāo	cake	蛋糕	11
	到	dào	to go to, to arrive	到	11
	到前面來	dào qiánmiàn lái	come to the front	到前面来	2
	德國	Déguó	Germany	德国	8
	德語	Déyǔ	German language	德语	8
	的	de	[possessive particle]	的	5
	得	de	[used after a verb to indicate degree or result]	得	8
	等於	děng yú	be equal to	等于	3
	弟弟	dìdi	younger brother	弟弟	6
	第二	dì èr	second	第二	3
	第二課	dì èr kè	lesson two	第二课	3
	第三	dì sān	third	第三	3
	第三課	dì sān kè	lesson three	第三课	3
	第一	dì yī	first	第一	3
	第一課	dì yī kè	lesson one	第一课	3
	點	diǎn	a little, a bit (short form of yìdiǎn 一點)	点	11
	東西	dōngxī	thing	东西	11
	動物	dòngwù	animal	动物	7
	都	dōu	all	都	7
	短	duǎn	short	短	10
	對不起	duìbùqǐ	excuse me, sorry	对不起	8
E	俄羅斯	Èluósī	Russia	俄罗斯	8
	餓	è	hungry	饿	11
	鱷魚	èyú	crocodile	鳄鱼	7
	兒子	érzi	son	儿子	6
	耳朵	ěrduǒ	ear	耳朵	10
	二	èr	two	二	3
F	法國	Fàguó	France	法国	8
	非常好	fēicháng hǎo	extremely good	非常好	2
	菲律賓	Fēilùbīn	the Philippines	菲律宾	8

	Traditional	Pinyin	English	Simplified	Lesson
	粉筆	fěnbǐ	chalk	粉笔	5
G	橄欖球	gǎnlǎnqiú	rugby	橄榄球	9
	高爾夫球	gāo'ěrfūqiú	golf	高尔夫球	9
	哥哥	gēge	elder brother	哥哥	6
	個	ge	[measure word]	个	6
	工人	gōngrén	laborer, worker	工人	6
	狗	gǒu	dog	狗	7
	姑姑	gūgu	father's sister	姑姑	6
	咕咾肉	gūlǎoròu	sweet and sour pork, a Cantonese dish	古老肉	11
	咕嚕肉	gūlūròu	sweet and sour pork, a Cantonese dish	咕噜肉	11
	國	guó	country	国	8
	果汁	guǒzhī	juice	果汁	11
H	漢堡	hànbǎo	hamburger (used in Taiwan)	汉堡	11
	漢堡包	hànbǎobāo	hamburger (used in China)	汉堡包	11
	漢語	Hànyǔ	Chinese language	汉语	8
	好	hǎo	good, well	好	2
	好啊	hǎo a	good! (agreeing)	好啊	9
	好嗎	hǎo ma	OK? (asking for agreement)	好吗	9
	喝	hē	to drink	喝	11
	和	hé, hàn	and	和	5
	黑板	hēibǎn	blackboard	黑板	5
	黑板擦	hēibǎncā	blackboard eraser	黑板擦	5
	很	hěn	very	很	7
	很好	hěn haǒ	very good	很好	2
	猴子	hóuzi	monkey	猴子	7
	蝴蝶	húdié	butterfly	蝴蝶	7
	護士	hùshì	nurse	护士	6
	歡迎	huānyíng	welcome	欢迎	4
	黃油	huángyóu	butter, also called nǎiyóu 奶油	黄油	11
	會	huì	can, to be able to	会	8
J	雞	jī	chicken, rooster	鸡	7
	幾	jǐ	how many	几	4
	繼父	jìfù	stepfather	继父	6
	繼母	jìmǔ	stepmother	继母	6
	家	jiā	family, home	家	6
	加	jiā	plus, to add	加	3
	加拿大	Jiānádà	Canada	加拿大	8
	減	jiǎn	minus, to subtract	减	3
	剪刀	jiǎndāo	scissors	剪刀	5
	見	jiàn	to see	见	2
	膠水	jiāoshuǐ	glue	胶水	5
	叫	jiào	to be called, to call	叫	6
	教室	jiàoshì	classroom	教室	5
	姊姊, 姐姐	jiějie	elder sister	姐姐	6

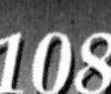

	Traditional	Pinyin	English	Simplified	Lesson
	今年	jīnnián	this year	今年	4
	金魚	jīnyú	goldfish	金鱼	7
	九	jiǔ	nine	九	3
	舅舅	jiùjiu	mother's brother	舅舅	6
K	開水	kāishuǐ	drinking water, boiled water	开水	11
	看	kàn	to look, to see	看	11
	看黑板	kàn hēibǎn	look at the blackboard	看黑板	2
	渴	kě	thirsty	渴	11
	可愛	kě'ài	lovely	可爱	7
	可樂	kělè	cola	可乐	11
	可是	kěshì	but	可是	11
	口	kǒu	mouth	口	1
	快樂	kuàilè	happy	快乐	4
	筷子	kuàizi	chopsticks	筷子	11
L	蘭蘭	Lánlán	a given name	兰兰	2
	籃球	lánqiú	basketball	篮球	9
	老虎	lǎohǔ	tiger	老虎	7
	老師	lǎoshī	teacher	老师	2
	老鼠	lǎoshǔ	mouse, rat	老鼠	7
	壘球	lěiqiú	softball	垒球	9
	李	Lǐ	a family name; lǐ- plum	李	2
	麗麗	Lìlì	Lily	丽丽	6
	臉	liǎn	face	脸	10
	兩	liǎng	two	两	4
	林	Lín	a family name; lín-forest	林	2
	〇	líng	zero	〇	3
	六	liù	six	六	3
	龍	lóng	dragon	龙	7
M	媽媽	māma	mom, mother	妈妈	6
	馬	mǎ	horse	马	7
	馬克	Mǎkè	Mark	马克	4
	馬來西亞	Mǎláixīyǎ	Malaysia	马来西亚	8
	螞蟻	mǎyǐ	ant	蚂蚁	7
	嗎	ma	[question word]	吗	5
	忙	máng	busy	忙	9
	貓	māo	cat	猫	7
	毛筆	máobǐ	writing brush	毛笔	5
	沒	méi	[negative word]	没	6
	沒關係	méi guānxì	it doesn't matter, that's all right	没关系	8
	沒有	méi yǒu	not have	没有	6
	眉毛	méimáo	eyebrow	眉毛	10
	美國	Měiguó	America, USA	美国	8
	美怡	Měiyí	a given name	美怡	10
	妹妹	mèimei	younger sister	妹妹	6

	Traditional	Pinyin	English	Simplified	Lesson
	門	mén	door	门	5
	們	men	[plural word]	们	2
	蜜蜂	mìfēng	bee	蜜蜂	7
	麵	miàn	noodles	面	11
	麵包	miànbāo	bread	面包	11
	明天	míngtiān	tomorrow	明天	2
	名字	míngzi	name	名字	6
	墨西哥	Mòxīgē	Mexico	墨西哥	8
N	拿	ná	to take, to hold	拿	11
	哪	nǎ	which	哪	8
	哪裡	nǎlǐ	not at all (said when praised; literally where)	哪里	8
	那	nà	that	那	5
	奶奶	nǎinai	grandma, grandmother	奶奶	6
	奶油	nǎiyóu	butter, also called huángyóu 黃油	奶油	11
	南非	Nánfēi	South Africa	南非	8
	呢	ne	[question word]	呢	6
	你	nǐ	you (singular)	你	2
	你的	nǐ de	your, yours	你的	5
	你好	nǐ hǎo	hello, how do you do	你好	2
	你們	nǐmen	you (plural)	你们	2
	年級	niánjí	grade	年级	10
	鳥	niǎo	bird	鸟	7
	檸檬雞片	níngméng-jīpiàn	lemon chicken	柠檬鸡片	11
	牛	niú	cow, ox	牛	7
	牛奶	niúnǎi	milk	牛奶	11
	紐西蘭	Niǔxīlán	New Zealand (used in Taiwan)	纽西兰	8
	女兒	nǚ'ér	daughter	女儿	6
P	排球	páiqiú	volleyball	排球	9
	跑步	pǎobù	running, to jog	跑步	9
	跑來跑去	pǎolái-pǎoqù	to run around	跑来跑去	7
	朋友	péngyǒu	friend	朋友	10
	匹	pī	[measure word for horses]	匹	7
	乒乓球	pīngpāngqiú	table tennis	乒乓球	9
Q	七	qī	seven	七	3
	妻子	qīzi	wife	妻子	6
	騎車	qíchē	cycling, to ride a bicycle	骑车	9
	汽水	qìshuǐ	soda pop	汽水	11
	鉛筆	qiānbǐ	pencil	铅笔	5
	鉛筆盒	qiānbǐhé	pencil case	铅笔盒	5
	巧克力	qiǎokèlì	chocolate	巧克力	11
	請安靜	qǐng ānjìng	quiet please	请安静	2
	請回座位	qǐng huí zuòwèi	return to (your) seat please	请回座位	2
	請進	qǐng jìn	come in please	请进	2
	請舉手	qǐng jǔshǒu	please raise (your) hand	请举手	2

	Traditional	Pinyin	English	Simplified	Lesson
	請坐	qǐng zuò	sit down please	请坐	2
	請坐好	qǐng zuò hǎo	sit properly please	请坐好	2
	請問	qǐngwèn	may I ask	请问	8
	曲棍球	qūgùnqiú	hockey	曲棍球	9
	去	qù	to go	去	9
	全家	quánjiā	whole family	全家	11
R	熱狗	règǒu	hotdog	热狗	11
	人	rén	person, people	人	1
	日本	Rìběn	Japan	日本	8
	日語	Rìyǔ	Japanese language	日语	8
	乳酪	rǔlào, rǔluò	cheese	乳酪	11
	瑞士	Ruìshì	Switzerland	瑞士	8
S	三	sān	three	三	3
	三明治	sānmíngzhì	sandwich	三明治	11
	山	shān	mountain	山	1
	上	shàng	to go, to attend; up	上	10
	蛇	shé	snake, serpent	蛇	7
	誰	shéi	who, whom	谁	4
	誰的	shéi de	whose	谁的	5
	什麼	shéme	what	什么	5
	生日	shēngrì	birthday	生日	4
	十	shí	ten	十	3
	是	shì	am, is, are	是	2
	是啊	shì a	yes, yeah (shows agreement)	是啊	7
	是的	shìde	yes (alternative of shì 是 in answering question)	是的	5
	書	shū	book	书	5
	書包	shūbāo	school bag	书包	5
	叔叔	shúshu	father's younger brother	叔叔	6
	薯條	shǔtiáo	French fries	薯条	11
	樹熊	shùxióng	koala (used in China)	树熊	3
	水	shuǐ	water	水	11
	說	shuō	to speak, to say	说	8
	說話	shuōhuà	to talk, to speak, to say	说话	10
	四	sì	four	四	3
	歲	suì	year of age	岁	4
T	他	tā	he, him	他	2
	她	tā	she, her	她	4
	牠	tā	it (animal)	它	7
	它	tā	it (object, item)	它	7
	牠們, 它們	tāmen	they (plural of it)	它们	7
	台灣	Táiwān	Taiwan	台湾	8
	太好了	tài hǎo le	that's great!	太好了	11
	太太	tàitai	Mrs, wife	太太	6
	泰國	Tàiguó	Thailand	泰国	8

Traditional	Pinyin	English	Simplified	Lesson
湯	tāng	soup	汤	11
踢	tī	to kick, to play (soccer)	踢	9
體操	tǐcāo	gymnastics	体操	9
田徑	tiánjìng	track and field	田径	9
條	tiáo	[measure word for long, thin objects]	条	7
跳高	tiàogāo	high jump	跳高	9
跳遠	tiàoyuǎn	long jump	跳远	9
同班	tóngbān	same class	同班	10
同學	tóngxué	fellow student, schoolmate	同学	2
同學們	tóngxuémen	fellow students (plural)	同学们	2
頭	tóu	head	头	10
頭髮	tóufǎ	hair (on human head)	头发	10
兔子	tùzi	rabbit, hare	兔子	7
W 王	Wáng	a family name; wáng- king	王	10
網球	wǎngqiú	tennis	网球	9
喂	wèi	hey!	喂	9
蚊子	wénzi	mosquito	蚊子	7
我	wǒ	I, me	我	2
我的	wǒ de	my, mine	我的	5
我們走吧	wǒmen zǒu ba	let's go	我们走吧	9
無尾熊	wúwěixióng	koala (used in Taiwan)	无尾熊	7
五	wǔ	five	五	3
X 西班牙	Xībānyá	Spain	西班牙	8
希臘	Xīlà	Greece	希腊	8
喜歡	xǐhuān	to like	喜欢	9
先生	xiānshēng	Mr, husband	先生	6
香港	Xiānggǎng	Hong Kong	香港	8
想	xiǎng	to feel like, to think	想	11
橡皮	xiàngpí	eraser	橡皮	5
小	xiǎo	small, little (in size)	小	7
小妹妹	xiǎo mèimei	little girl	小妹妹	8
小明	Xiǎomíng	a given name	小明	5
笑哈哈	xiàohāhā	to laugh heartily, laughingly	笑哈哈	10
謝謝	xièxie	thanks	谢谢	4
新加坡	Xīnjiāpō	Singapore	新加坡	8
新幾內亞	Xīnjǐnèiyǎ	New Guinea	新几内亚	8
新西蘭	Xīnxīlán	New Zealand (used in China)	新西兰	8
姓	xìng	family name, surname	姓	6
凶	xiōng	fierce, ferocious	凶	7
凶巴巴	xiōngbābā	fiercely, ferociously	凶巴巴	10
熊貓	xióngmāo	panda	熊猫	7
學生	xuéshēng	student, pupil	学生	6
學校	xuéxiào	school	学校	10
Y 鴨子	yāzi	duck	鸭子	7

Traditional	Pinyin	English	Simplified	Lesson
眼睛	yǎnjīng	eye	眼睛	10
羊	yáng	goat, ram	羊	7
爺爺	yéye	granddad, grandfather	爷爷	6
也	yě	also, too	也	6
一	yī	one	一	3
一點	yìdiǎn	a little, a bit	一点	8
醫生	yīshēng	doctor	医生	6
姨	yí	mother's sister	姨	6
咦	yí	why!, huh! (indicating surprise)	咦	8
椅子	yǐzi	chair	椅子	5
義大利	Yìdàlì	Italy	意大利	8
印度	Yìndù	India	印度	8
英國	Yīngguó	England	英国	8
英語	Yīngyǔ	English language	英语	8
游泳	yóuyǒng	swimming, to swim	游泳	9
有	yǒu	to have, there is/are	有	6
魚	yú	fish	鱼	7
圓珠筆	yuánzhūbǐ	ballpoint pen (used in China)	圆珠笔	5
原子筆	yuánzǐbǐ	ballpoint pen (used in Taiwan)	原子笔	5
越南	Yuènán	Vietnam	越南	8
運動	yùndòng	sports, exercise	运动	9
Z 再見	zàijiàn	goodbye	再见	2
再說一次	zài shuō yí cì	say (it) again	再说一次	2
早	zǎo	morning, early	早	2
炸蝦片	zháxiāpiàn	prawn crackers	炸虾片	11
站起來	zhàn qǐlái	stand up	站起来	2
蟑螂	zhāngláng	cockroach	蟑螂	7
丈夫	zhàngfū	husband	丈夫	6
這	zhè	this	这	5
真	zhēn	really	真	7
真的啊	zhēnde a	really!	真的啊	11
隻	zhī	[measure word for dogs, cats, birds]	只	7
知道	zhīdào	to know	知道	5
紙	zhǐ	paper	纸	5
中國	Zhōngguó	China	中国	8
中文	Zhōngwén	Chinese language	中文	8
豬	zhū	pig, boar	猪	7
祝	zhù	to wish (offer good wishes)	祝	4
注意聽	zhùyì tīng	listen carefully	注意听	2
桌子	zhuōzi	desk	桌子	5
走	zǒu	to go, to walk	走	9
走吧	zǒu ba	let's go!	走吧	9
足球	zúqiú	soccer	足球	9
嘴巴	zuǐbā	mouth	嘴巴	10
最	zuì	most	最	9
做	zuò	to make, to cook, to do	做	11

WORDS AND EXPRESSIONS
English-Chinese

English	Pinyin	Traditional
Grammar:		
degree or result	de	得
exclamation	a	啊
negative word	bù	不
	méi	沒
possessive particle	de	的
question word	ma	嗎
	ne	呢
suggestion	ba	吧
Plural form:		
	men	們
Measure words:		
dogs, cats, birds	zhī	隻
fish	tiáo	條
horses	pī	匹
people	ge	個
Family names:		
	Bái	白
	Lǐ	李
	Lín	林
	Mǎ	馬
	Shānkǒu	山口 (Japanese)
	Wáng	王
Given names:		
	Dàlì	大利
	Dàmíng	大明
	Dàzhōng	大中
	Guómíng	國明
	Jiǔshān	九山
	Lánlán	蘭蘭
	Měiyí	美怡
	Sānshān	三山
	Xiǎoguó	小國
	Xiǎomáo	小毛
	Xiǎoměi	小美
	Xiǎomíng	小明
David	Dàwěi	大偉
Lily	Lìlì	麗麗
Mark	Mǎkè	馬克
A		
a little, a bit	diǎn, yìdiǎn	點, 一點
a little louder	dà shēng yìdiǎn	大聲一點
able to, can	huì	會
age: year of-	suì	歲
all	dōu	都
also, too	yě	也
am, is, are	shì	是
am not, is not, are not	bú shì	不是
America, USA	Měiguó	美國
and	hé, hàn	和
animal	dòngwù	動物
ant	mǎyǐ	螞蟻
are, is, am	shì	是
are not	bú shì	不是
arrive, to go to	dào	到
attend (school, work)	shàng	上
aunt (father's sister)	gūgu	姑姑
(mother's sister)	āyí	阿姨
Australia (in Taiwan)	Àozhōu	澳洲
(in China)	Àodàlìyà	澳大利亞
B		
badminton	yǔmáoqiú	羽毛球
ballpoint pen	yuánzǐbǐ	原子筆
baseball	bàngqiú	棒球
basketball	lánqiú	籃球
bat	biǎnfú	蝙蝠
bee	mìfēng	蜜蜂
big, large	dà	大
bird	niǎo	鳥
birthday	shēngrì	生日
blackboard	hēibǎn	黑板
blackboard eraser	hēibǎncā	黑板擦
boar, pig	zhū	豬
boiled water	kāishuǐ	開水
book	shū	書
bowling: tenpin-	bǎolíngqiú	保齡球
bread	miànbāo	麵包
brother: elder-	gēge	哥哥
brother: younger-	dìdi	弟弟
brush : writing-	máobǐ	毛筆
busy	máng	忙
but	kěshì	可是
butter	huángyóu, nǎiyóu	黃油, 奶油
butterfly	húdié	蝴蝶
C		
cake	dàngāo	蛋糕
call (*v.*), to be called	jiào	叫

English	Pinyin	Traditional
can, to be able to	huì	會
Canada	Jiānádà	加拿大
Canadian	Jiānádàrén	加拿大人
cannot, unable to	bú huì	不會
cat	māo	貓
chair	yǐzi	椅子
chalk	fěnbǐ	粉筆
cheese	rǔlào, rǔluò	乳酪
chicken, rooster	jī	雞
China	Zhōngguó	中國
Chinese language	Zhōngwén, Hànyǔ	中文，漢語
(in China)	Pǔtōnghuà	普通話
(in Taiwan)	Guóyǔ	國語
Chinese (person)	Zhōngguórén	中國人
chocolate	qiǎokèlì	巧克力
chopsticks	kuàizi	筷子
Christian name	míngzi	名字
classroom	jiàoshì	教室
cockroach	zhāngláng	蟑螂
cola	kělè	可樂
color pencil	cǎisèbǐ	彩色筆
come in please	qǐng jìn	請進
come to the front	dào qiánmiàn lái	到前面來
cook (*v.*), to make	zuò	做
cookies	bǐnggān	餅乾
country	guó	國
cow, ox	niú	牛
cricket	bǎnqiú	板球
crocodile	èyú	鱷魚
cycling, ride a bicycle	qíchē	騎車

D

English	Pinyin	Traditional
dad, father	bàba	爸爸
daughter	nǚ'ér	女兒
David	Dàwěi	大偉
desk	zhuōzi	桌子
dish, meal, vegetable	cài	菜
divided by	chú yǐ	除以
do, to make, to cook	zuò	做
do not talk	bú yào shuōhuà	不要說話
doctor	yīshēng	醫生
dog	gǒu	狗
don't mention it,	bú kèqì,	不客氣，
you are welcome	bié kèqì	別客氣
door	mén	門
dragon	lóng	龍
drink (*v.*)	hē	喝
drinking water	kāishuǐ	開水
duck	yāzi	鴨子

E

English	Pinyin	Traditional
ear	ěrduǒ	耳朵
early, morning	zǎo	早
eat	chī	吃
eight	bā	八
elder brother	gēge	哥哥
elder sister	jiějie	姊姊，姐姐
England	Yīngguó	英國
English language	Yīngyǔ	英語
Englishman	Yīngguórén	英國人
equal to	děngyú	等於
eraser	xiàngpí	橡皮
excuse me, sorry	duìbùqǐ	對不起
exercise, sports	yùndòng	運動
extremely good	fēicháng hǎo	非常好
eye	yǎnjīng	眼睛
eyebrow	méimáo	眉毛

F

English	Pinyin	Traditional
face	liǎn	臉
family, home	jiā	家
family name	xìng	姓
father, dad	bàba	爸爸
father's elder brother	bóbo	伯伯
father's sister	gūgu	姑姑
father's younger brother	shúshu	叔叔
feel like, to think	xiǎng	想
fellow student	tóngxué	同學
fellow students	tóngxuémen	同學們
ferocious, fierce	xiōng,	凶，
ferociously, fiercely	xiōngbābā	凶巴巴
first	dì yī	第一
first name	míngzi	名字
fish	yú	魚
five	wǔ	五
fly (*n.*)	cāngyíng	蒼蠅
four	sì	四
France	Fàguó	法國
French fries	shǔtiáo	薯條
fried rice	chǎofàn	炒飯
friend	péngyǒu	朋友

G

English	Pinyin	Traditional
German language	Déyǔ	德語
German (person)	Déguórén	德國人
Germany	Déguó	德國
glue	jiāoshuǐ	膠水
go	qù	去
go, to attend; up	shàng	上
go, to walk	zǒu	走

English	Pinyin	Traditional
go to, to arrive	dào	到
goat, ram	yáng	羊
goldfish	jīnyú	金魚
golf	gāo'ěrfūqiú	高爾夫球
good! (agreeing)	hǎo a	好啊
good, well	hǎo	好
goodbye	zàijiàn	再見
grade (school)	niánjí	年級
granddad	yéye	爺爺
grandma	nǎinai	奶奶
Greece	Xīlà	希臘
gymnastics	tǐcāo	體操

H

English	Pinyin	Traditional
hair (on human head)	tóufǎ	頭髮
hamburger (in Taiwan)	hànbǎo	漢堡
(in China)	hànbǎobāo	漢堡包
happy	kuàilè	快樂
have/has	yǒu	有
have a meal	chīfàn	吃飯
he, him	tā	他
head	tóu	頭
hello, how do you do	nǐ hǎo	你好
her	tāde	她的
her, she	tā	她
hers	tā de	她的
hey!	wèi	喂
high jump	tiàogāo	跳高
him, he	tā	他
his	tā de	他的
hit	dǎ	打
hockey	qūgùnqiú	曲棍球
hold, to take	ná	拿
home, family	jiā	家
Hong Kong	Xiānggǎng	香港
horse	mǎ	馬
hotdog	règǒu	熱狗
how do you do, hello	nǐ hǎo	你好
how many	jǐ	幾
huh! (surprise)	yí	咦
hundred	bǎi	百
hungry	è	餓
husband	zhàngfū	丈夫
husband, Mr	xiānshēng	先生

I

English	Pinyin	Traditional
I, me	wǒ	我
ice cream	bīngqílín	冰淇淋
India	Yìndù	印度
Ireland	Ài'ěrlán	愛爾蘭
is, are, am	shì	是
is not	búshì	不是
it	tā	它, 牠
it doesn't matter	méi guānxì	沒關係
Italy	Yìdàlì	義大利
its	tāde	它的, 牠的

J

English	Pinyin	Traditional
Japan	Rìběn	日本
Japanese language	Rìyǔ	日語
Japanese (person)	Rìběnrén	日本人
jogging, running	pǎobù	跑步
juice	guǒzhī	果汁

K

English	Pinyin	Traditional
kangaroo	dàishǔ	袋鼠
kick	tī	踢
know	zhīdào	知道
koala (in Taiwan)	wúwěixióng	無尾熊
(in China)	kǎolā, shùxióng	考拉, 樹熊

L

English	Pinyin	Traditional
laborer, worker	gōngrén	工人
large, big	dà	大
laughingly	xiàohāhā	笑哈哈
lemon chicken	níngméng-jīpiàn	檸檬雞片
lesson one	dì yī kè	第一課
lesson three	dì sān kè	第三課
lesson two	dì èr kè	第二課
let's go	wǒmen zǒu ba	我們走吧
like (*v.*)	xǐhuān	喜歡
listen carefully	zhùyì tīng	注意聽
little (in size), small	xiǎo	小
little: a-, a bit	yìdiǎn	一點
little girl	xiǎo mèimei	小妹妹
long	cháng	長
long jump	tiàoyuǎn	跳遠
look, to see	kàn	看
look at the blackboard	kàn hēibǎn	看黑板
louder: a little-	dà shēng yìdiǎn	大聲一點
lovely	kě'ài	可愛

M

English	Pinyin	Traditional
make, to cook, to do	zuò	做
Malaysia	Mǎláixīyǎ	馬來西亞
Mark	Mǎkè	馬克
may I ask	qǐngwèn	請問
me, I	wǒ	我
meal, dish, vegetable	cài	菜
meal: to have a-	chī fàn	吃飯
Mexico	Mòxīgē	墨西哥
milk (cow)	niúnǎi	牛奶

English	Pinyin	Traditional
mine, my	wǒ de	我的
minus	jiǎn	減
monkey	hóuzi	猴子
morning, early	zǎo	早
mosquito	wénzi	蚊子
most	zuì	最
mother, mom	māma	媽媽
mother's sister	yí	姨
(in Taiwan)	āyí	阿姨
mother's brother	jiùjiu	舅舅
mountain	shān	山
mouse, rat	lǎoshǔ	老鼠
mouth	kǒu,	口,
	zuǐbā	嘴巴
Mr, husband	xiānshēng	先生
Mrs, wife	tàitai	太太
multiplied by	chéng yǐ	乘以
my, mine	wǒ de	我的
N		
name	míngzi	名字
New Guinea	Xīnjǐnèiyǎ	新幾內亞
New Zealand (in China)	Xīnxīlán	新西蘭
(in Taiwan)	Niǔxīlán	紐西蘭
New Zealander	Xīnxīlánrén	紐西蘭人
nine	jiǔ	九
no	bú shì	不是
noodles	miàn	麵
nose	bízi	鼻子
not (to form negative)	bù	不
not at all (when praised)	nǎlǐ	哪裡
(when thanked)	bú kèqì	不客氣
not going	bú qù	不去
not have	méi yǒu	沒有
nurse	hùshì	護士
O		
OK?	hǎo ma	好嗎
one	yī	一
open (your) book	bǎ shū dǎkāi	把書打開
P		
panda	xióngmāo	熊貓
paper	zhǐ	紙
Paul	Bǎoluó	保羅
pen	bǐ	筆
pencil	qiānbǐ	鉛筆
pencil case	qiānbǐhé	鉛筆盒
people, person	rén	人
pet	chǒngwù	寵物
Philippines	Fēilùbīn	菲律賓

English	Pinyin	Traditional
pig, boar	zhū	豬
play (basketball, tennis)	dǎ	打
(soccer)	tī	踢
plus	jiā	加
prawn crackers	zháxiāpiàn	炸蝦片
probably	dàgài	大概
pupil, student	xuéshēng	學生
put down (your) hand	bǎ shǒu fàng xià	把手放下
Q		
quiet please	qǐng ānjìng	請安靜
R		
rabbit, hare	tùzi	兔子
raise (your) hand plse.	qǐng jǔshǒu	請舉手
rat, mouse	lǎoshǔ	老鼠
really	zhēn	真
really!	zhēnde a!	真的啊！
return to (your) seat plse.	qǐng huí zuòwèi	請回座位
ride a bicycle	qíchē	騎車
rugby	gǎnlǎnqiú	橄欖球
ruler (measure)	chǐ	尺
run around	pǎolái-pǎoqù	跑來跑去
running, to jog	pǎobù	跑步
Russia	Èluósī	俄羅斯
S		
same class	tóngbān	同班
sandwich	sānmíngzhì	三明治
say, talk	shuōhuà	說話
say (it) again	zài shuō yí cì	再說一次
school	xuéxiào	學校
school bag	shūbāo	書包
schoolmate	tóngxué	同學
schoolmates	tóngxuémen	同學們
scissors	jiǎndāo	剪刀
second	dì èr	第二
see, catch sight of	jiàn	見
see, look	kàn	看
seven	qī	七
she, her	tā	她
short	duǎn	短
Singapore	Xīnjiāpō	新加坡
sister (elder)	jiějie	姊姊, 姐姐
(younger)	mèimei	妹妹
sit down please	qǐng zuò	請坐
sit properly please	qǐng zuò hǎo	請坐好
six	liù	六
small	xiǎo	小
snake, serpent	shé	蛇
soccer	zúqiú	足球

English	Pinyin	Traditional
soda pop	qìshuǐ	汽水
softball	lěiqiú	壘球
son	érzi	兒子
sorry, excuse me	duìbùqǐ	對不起
soup	tāng	湯
South Africa	Nánfēi	南非
Spain	Xībānyá	西班牙
speak	shuō,	說,
	shuōhuà	說話
sports, exercise	yùndòng	運動
spring rolls	chūnjuǎn	春捲
stand up	zhàn qǐlái	站起來
stepfather	jìfù	繼父
stepmother	jìmǔ	繼母
student	xuéshēng	學生
surname	xìng	姓
sweet and sour pork	gūlǎoròu,	咕咾肉,
	gūlūròu	咕嚕肉
swimming, to swim	yóuyǒng	游泳
Switzerland	Ruìshì	瑞士
T		
table tennis	pīngpāngqiú	乒乓球
Taiwan	Táiwān	台灣
take, to hold	ná	拿
talk	shuōhuà	說話
teacher	lǎoshī	老師
ten	shí	十
tennis	wǎngqiú	網球
Thailand	Tàiguó	泰國
thank you	xièxie nǐ	謝謝你
thanks	xièxie	謝謝
that	nà	那
that's all right, it doesn't matter	méi guānxì	沒關係
that's great!	tài hǎo le	太好了
there is/are	yǒu	有
they (people)	tāmen	他們
(animal)	tāmen	牠們
(object)	tāmen	它們
thing	dōngxī	東西
think, feel like	xiǎng	想
third	dì sān	第三
thirsty	kě	渴
this	zhè	這
this year	jīnnián	今年
three	sān	三
tiger	lǎohǔ	老虎
tomorrow	míngtiān	明天
too, also	yě	也
track and field	tiánjìng	田徑
two	èr, liǎng	二, 兩
U		
unable to, cannot	bú huì	不會
uncle (mother's brother)	jiùjiu	舅舅
(father's elder brother)	bóbo	伯伯
(father's younger brother)	shúshu	叔叔
USA, America	Měiguó	美國
V		
vegetable, dish, meal	cài	菜
very	hěn	很
very good	hěn haǒ	很好
Vietnam	Yuènán	越南
volleyball	páiqiú	排球
W		
water	shuǐ	水
welcome	huānyíng	歡迎
well, good	hǎo	好
what	shéme	什麼
which	nǎ	哪
white	bái	白
who, whom	shéi	誰
whole family	quánjiā	全家
whose	shéi de	誰的
why!, huh! (indicating surprise)	yí	咦
wife	qīzi	妻子
wife, Mrs	tàitai	太太
window	chuānghù	窗户
wish (offer good wishes)	zhù	祝
writing brush	máobǐ	毛筆
Y		
year of age	suì	歲
yes	shìde	是的
yes!	shì a	是啊
you (singular)	nǐ	你
(plural)	nǐmen	你們
(polite)	nín	您
you're welcome	bié kèqì,	別客氣,
	bú kèqì	不客氣
younger brother	dìdi	弟弟
younger sister	mèimei	妹妹
your, yours	nǐ de	你的
Z		
zero	líng	〇

拼音、注音符號對照表

注音符號		ㄚ	ㄛ	ㄜ	ㄞ	ㄟ	ㄠ	ㄡ	ㄢ	ㄣ	ㄤ	ㄥ	ㄦ	ㄧ	ㄧㄚ	ㄧㄝ	ㄧㄠ	ㄧㄡ
	拼音	**a**	**o**	**e**	**ai**	**ei**	**ao**	**ou**	**an**	**en**	**ang**	**eng**	**er**	**i**	**ia**	**ie**	**iao**	**iu**
		a 啊 ㄚ		è 餓 ㄜˋ	āi 唉 ㄞ		āo 凹 ㄠ	ōu 歐 ㄡ	ān 安 ㄢ	ēn 恩 ㄣ	áng 昂 ㄤˊ		ér 兒 ㄦˊ	yī 衣 ㄧ	yá 牙 ㄧㄚˊ	yě 也 ㄧㄝˇ	yào 要 ㄧㄠˋ	yòu 又 ㄧㄡˋ
ㄅ	**b**	bà 爸 ㄅㄚˋ	bó 伯 ㄅㄛˊ		bǎi 百 ㄅㄞˇ	běi 北 ㄅㄟˇ	bào 報 ㄅㄠˋ		bàn 半 ㄅㄢˋ	běn 本 ㄅㄣˇ	bāng 幫 ㄅㄤ	bēng 崩 ㄅㄥ		bǐ 筆 ㄅㄧˇ		bié 別 ㄅㄧㄝˊ	biǎo 錶 ㄅㄧㄠˇ	
ㄆ	**p**	pà 怕 ㄆㄚˋ	pò 破 ㄆㄛˋ		pái 排 ㄆㄞˊ	péi 陪 ㄆㄟˊ	pǎo 跑 ㄆㄠˇ	pǒu 剖 ㄆㄡˇ	pán 盤 ㄆㄢˊ	pén 盆 ㄆㄣˊ	páng 旁 ㄆㄤˊ	péng 朋 ㄆㄥˊ		pí 皮 ㄆㄧˊ		piě 撇 ㄆㄧㄝˇ	piào 票 ㄆㄧㄠˋ	
ㄇ	**m**	mǎ 馬 ㄇㄚˇ	mò 墨 ㄇㄛˋ		mǎi 買 ㄇㄞˇ	mèi 妹 ㄇㄟˋ	máo 毛 ㄇㄠˊ	móu 謀 ㄇㄡˊ	màn 慢 ㄇㄢˋ	mén 門 ㄇㄣˊ	máng 忙 ㄇㄤˊ	méng 檬 ㄇㄥˊ		mǐ 米 ㄇㄧˇ		miè 滅 ㄇㄧㄝˋ	miǎo 秒 ㄇㄧㄠˇ	miù 謬 ㄇㄧㄡˋ
ㄈ	**f**	fǎ 法 ㄈㄚˇ	fó 佛 ㄈㄛˊ			fēi 非 ㄈㄟ		fǒu 否 ㄈㄡˇ	fàn 飯 ㄈㄢˋ	fēn 分 ㄈㄣ	fáng 房 ㄈㄤˊ	fēng 風 ㄈㄥ						
ㄉ	**d**	dà 大 ㄉㄚˋ		de 的 ˙ㄉㄜ	dài 帶 ㄉㄞˋ	děi 得 ㄉㄟˇ	dào 到 ㄉㄠˋ	dōu 都 ㄉㄡ	dàn 但 ㄉㄢˋ		dāng 當 ㄉㄤ	děng 等 ㄉㄥˇ		dì 弟 ㄉㄧˋ		dié 碟 ㄉㄧㄝˊ	diào 釣 ㄉㄧㄠˋ	diū 丟 ㄉㄧㄡ
ㄊ	**t**	tā 他 ㄊㄚ		tè 特 ㄊㄜˋ	tài 太 ㄊㄞˋ		tào 套 ㄊㄠˋ	tóu 頭 ㄊㄡˊ	tán 談 ㄊㄢˊ		tāng 湯 ㄊㄤ	téng 疼 ㄊㄥˊ		tǐ 體 ㄊㄧˇ		tiē 貼 ㄊㄧㄝ	tiáo 條 ㄊㄧㄠˊ	
ㄋ	**n**	nà 那 ㄋㄚˋ		ne 呢 ˙ㄋㄜ	nǎi 奶 ㄋㄞˇ	nèi 內 ㄋㄟˋ	nǎo 腦 ㄋㄠˇ	nòu 耨 ㄋㄡˋ	nán 男 ㄋㄢˊ	nèn 嫩 ㄋㄣˋ	náng 囊 ㄋㄤˊ	néng 能 ㄋㄥˊ		nǐ 你 ㄋㄧˇ		niē 捏 ㄋㄧㄝ	niǎo 鳥 ㄋㄧㄠˇ	niú 牛 ㄋㄧㄡˊ
ㄌ	**l**	là 辣 ㄌㄚˋ		lè 樂 ㄌㄜˋ	lái 來 ㄌㄞˊ	léi 雷 ㄌㄟˊ	lǎo 老 ㄌㄠˇ	lóu 樓 ㄌㄡˊ	lán 蘭 ㄌㄢˊ		láng 狼 ㄌㄤˊ	lěng 冷 ㄌㄥˇ		lì 麗 ㄌㄧˋ	liǎ 倆 ㄌㄧㄚˇ	liè 列 ㄌㄧㄝˋ		liú 留 ㄌㄧㄡˊ
ㄍ	**g**	gà 尬 ㄍㄚˋ		gè 各 ㄍㄜˋ	gāi 該 ㄍㄞ	gěi 給 ㄍㄟˇ	gāo 高 ㄍㄠ	gǒu 狗 ㄍㄡˇ	gān 甘 ㄍㄢ	gēn 跟 ㄍㄣ	gāng 剛 ㄍㄤ	gèng 更 ㄍㄥˋ						
ㄎ	**k**	kǎ 卡 ㄎㄚˇ		kè 課 ㄎㄜˋ	kāi 開 ㄎㄞ		kǎo 考 ㄎㄠˇ	kǒu 口 ㄎㄡˇ	kàn 看 ㄎㄢˋ	kěn 肯 ㄎㄣˇ	kāng 康 ㄎㄤ	kēng 坑 ㄎㄥ						
ㄏ	**h**	hā 哈 ㄏㄚ		hē 喝 ㄏㄜ	héi 孩 ㄏㄞˊ	hēi 黑 ㄏㄟ	hǎo 好 ㄏㄠˇ	hòu 後 ㄏㄡˋ	hàn 漢 ㄏㄢˋ	hěn 很 ㄏㄣˇ	héng 杭 ㄏㄤˊ	héng 恆 ㄏㄥˊ						
ㄐ	**j**													jī 雞 ㄐㄧ	jiā 家 ㄐㄧㄚ	jiě 姊 ㄐㄧㄝˇ	jiào 叫 ㄐㄧㄠˋ	jiǔ 九 ㄐㄧㄡˇ
ㄑ	**q**													qǐ 起 ㄑㄧˇ	qià 恰 ㄑㄧㄚˋ	qiě 且 ㄑㄧㄝˇ	qiáo 橋 ㄑㄧㄠˊ	qiū 秋 ㄑㄧㄡ
ㄒ	**x**													xī 西 ㄒㄧ	xià 下 ㄒㄧㄚˋ	xiě 寫 ㄒㄧㄝˇ	xiǎo 小 ㄒㄧㄠˇ	xiū 休 ㄒㄧㄡ
ㄓ	**zh**	zhà 詐 ㄓㄚˋ	zhèi 這 ㄓㄟˋ	zhè 這 ㄓㄜˋ	zhǎi 窄 ㄓㄞˇ		zhǎo 找 ㄓㄠˇ	zhōu 周 ㄓㄡ	zhàn 站 ㄓㄢˋ	zhēn 真 ㄓㄣ	zhāng 張 ㄓㄤ	zhèng 正 ㄓㄥˋ		zhī 隻 ㄓ				
ㄔ	**ch**	chā 叉 ㄔㄚ		chē 車 ㄔㄜ	chāi 拆 ㄔㄞ		chǎo 炒 ㄔㄠˇ	chǒu 丑 ㄔㄡˇ	chǎn 產 ㄔㄢˇ	chén 陳 ㄔㄣˊ	cháng 常 ㄔㄤˊ	chéng 成 ㄔㄥˊ		chī 吃 ㄔ				
ㄕ	**sh**	shā 沙 ㄕㄚ		shè 射 ㄕㄜˋ	shài 曬 ㄕㄞˋ	shéi 誰 ㄕㄟˊ	shǎo 少 ㄕㄠˇ	shǒu 手 ㄕㄡˇ	shān 山 ㄕㄢ	shēn 身 ㄕㄣ	shàng 上 ㄕㄤˋ	shēng 生 ㄕㄥ		shì 是 ㄕˋ				
ㄖ	**r**			rè 熱 ㄖㄜˋ			rǎo 擾 ㄖㄠˇ	ròu 肉 ㄖㄡˋ	rán 然 ㄖㄢˊ	rén 人 ㄖㄣˊ	ràng 讓 ㄖㄤˋ	réng 仍 ㄖㄥˊ		rì 日 ㄖˋ				
ㄗ	**z**	zá 雜 ㄗㄚˊ		zé 則 ㄗㄜˊ	zài 在 ㄗㄞˋ	zéi 賊 ㄗㄟˊ	zǎo 早 ㄗㄠˇ	zǒu 走 ㄗㄡˇ	zán 咱 ㄗㄢˊ	zěn 怎 ㄗㄣˇ		zēng 增 ㄗㄥ		zì 字 ㄗˋ				
ㄘ	**c**	cā 擦 ㄘㄚ		cè 冊 ㄘㄜˋ	cài 菜 ㄘㄞˋ		cāo 操 ㄘㄠ	còu 湊 ㄘㄡˋ	cān 餐 ㄘㄢ	cén 岑 ㄘㄣˊ		céng 層 ㄘㄥˊ		cì 次 ㄘˋ				
ㄙ	**s**	sǎ 灑 ㄙㄚˇ		sè 色 ㄙㄜˋ	sài 賽 ㄙㄞˋ		sǎo 嫂 ㄙㄠˇ	sòu 嗽 ㄙㄡˋ	sān 三 ㄙㄢ	sēn 森 ㄙㄣ		sēng 僧 ㄙㄥ		sǐ 死 ㄙˇ				

Pinyin, Zhuyin-fuhao Chart

ㄧㄢ	ㄧㄣ	ㄧㄤ	ㄧㄥ	ㄩㄥ	ㄨ	ㄨㄚ	ㄨㄛ	ㄨㄞ	ㄨㄟ	ㄨㄢ	ㄨㄣ	ㄨㄤ	ㄨㄥ	ㄩ	ㄩㄝ	ㄩㄢ	ㄩㄣ	
ian	**in**	**iang**	**ing**	**iong**	**u**	**ua**	**uo**	**uai**	**ui**	**uan**	**un**	**uang**	**ong**	**ü**	**ue**	**uan**	**un**	
yán 言 ㄧㄢˊ	yīn 音 ㄧㄣ	yáng 洋 ㄧㄤˊ	yīng 英 ㄧㄥ	yòng 用 ㄩㄥˋ	wǔ 五 ㄨˇ	wá 娃 ㄨㄚˊ	wǒ 我 ㄨㄛˇ	wài 外 ㄨㄞˋ	wèi 位 ㄨㄟˋ	wǎn 晚 ㄨㄢˇ	wén 文 ㄨㄣˊ	wáng 王 ㄨㄤˊ	wōng 翁 ㄨㄥ	yǔ 雨 ㄩˇ	yuè 月 ㄩㄝˋ	yuán 元 ㄩㄢˊ	yún 雲 ㄩㄣˊ	
biān 邊 ㄅㄧㄢ	bīn 賓 ㄅㄧㄣ		bìng 病 ㄅㄧㄥˋ		bù 不 ㄅㄨˋ													**b**
piàn 片 ㄆㄧㄢˋ	pǐn 品 ㄆㄧㄣˇ		píng 平 ㄆㄧㄥˊ		pú 匍 ㄆㄨˊ													**p**
miàn 面 ㄇㄧㄢˋ	mín 民 ㄇㄧㄣˊ		míng 明 ㄇㄧㄥˊ		mǔ 母 ㄇㄨˇ													**m**
					fù 父 ㄈㄨˋ													**f**
diǎn 點 ㄉㄧㄢˇ			dìng 定 ㄉㄧㄥˋ		dù 度 ㄉㄨˋ		duō 多 ㄉㄨㄛ		duì 對 ㄉㄨㄟˋ	duǎn 短 ㄉㄨㄢˇ	dùn 盾 ㄉㄨㄣˋ		dōng 東 ㄉㄨㄥ					**d**
tiān 天 ㄊㄧㄢ			tīng 聽 ㄊㄧㄥ		tú 圖 ㄊㄨˊ		tuō 託 ㄊㄨㄛ		tuī 推 ㄊㄨㄟ	tuán 團 ㄊㄨㄢˊ	tūn 吞 ㄊㄨㄣ		tóng 同 ㄊㄨㄥˊ					**t**
nián 年 ㄋㄧㄢˊ	nín 您 ㄋㄧㄣˊ	niáng 娘 ㄋㄧㄤˊ	níng 檸 ㄋㄧㄥˊ		nǔ 努 ㄋㄨˇ		nuó 挪 ㄋㄨㄛˊ			nuǎn 暖 ㄋㄨㄢˇ			nóng 農 ㄋㄨㄥˊ	nǚ 女 ㄋㄩˇ	nuè 虐 ㄋㄩㄝˋ			**n**
lián 連 ㄌㄧㄢˊ	lín 林 ㄌㄧㄣˊ	liǎng 兩 ㄌㄧㄤˇ	líng 玲 ㄌㄧㄥˊ		lù 路 ㄌㄨˋ		luó 羅 ㄌㄨㄛˊ			luàn 亂 ㄌㄨㄢˋ	lùn 論 ㄌㄨㄣˋ		lóng 龍 ㄌㄨㄥˊ	lǜ 綠 ㄌㄩˋ	luè 略 ㄌㄩㄝˋ			**l**
					gū 姑 ㄍㄨ	guā 瓜 ㄍㄨㄚ	guó 國 ㄍㄨㄛˊ	guài 怪 ㄍㄨㄞˋ	guì 貴 ㄍㄨㄟˋ	guān 官 ㄍㄨㄢ	gùn 棍 ㄍㄨㄣˋ	guāng 光 ㄍㄨㄤ	gòng 共 ㄍㄨㄥˋ					**g**
					kū 哭 ㄎㄨ	kuā 誇 ㄎㄨㄚ	kuò 闊 ㄎㄨㄛˋ	kuài 塊 ㄎㄨㄞˋ	kuì 愧 ㄎㄨㄟˋ	kuān 寬 ㄎㄨㄢ	kūn 坤 ㄎㄨㄣ	kuàng 況 ㄎㄨㄤˋ	kòng 空 ㄎㄨㄥˋ					**k**
					hú 湖	huà 話 ㄏㄨㄚˋ	huó 活 ㄏㄨㄛˊ	huài 壞 ㄏㄨㄞˋ	huí 回 ㄏㄨㄟˊ	huān 歡 ㄏㄨㄢ	hūn 婚 ㄏㄨㄣ	huáng 黃 ㄏㄨㄤˊ	hóng 紅 ㄏㄨㄥˊ					**h**
jiàn 見 ㄐㄧㄢˋ	jīn 今 ㄐㄧㄣ	jiāng 江 ㄐㄧㄤ	jīng 睛 ㄐㄧㄥ	jiǒng 窘 ㄐㄩㄥˇ										jú 局	jué 決 ㄐㄩㄝˊ	juǎn 捲 ㄐㄩㄢˇ	jūn 君 ㄐㄩㄣ	**j**
qián 前 ㄑㄧㄢˊ	qín 琴 ㄑㄧㄣˊ	qiáng 強 ㄑㄧㄤˊ	qǐng 請 ㄑㄧㄥˇ	qióng 窮 ㄑㄩㄥˊ										qù 去 ㄑㄩˋ	quē 缺 ㄑㄩㄝ	quán 全 ㄑㄩㄢˊ	qún 裙 ㄑㄩㄣˊ	**q**
xiān 先 ㄒㄧㄢ	xīn 新 ㄒㄧㄣ	xiǎng 想 ㄒㄧㄤˇ	xīng 星 ㄒㄧㄥ	xióng 雄 ㄒㄩㄥˊ										xū 須 ㄒㄩ	xuě 雪 ㄒㄩㄝˇ	xuǎn 選 ㄒㄩㄢˇ	xún 尋 ㄒㄩㄣˊ	**x**
					zhù 祝 ㄓㄨˋ	zhuā 抓 ㄓㄨㄚ	zhuō 桌 ㄓㄨㄛ	zhuǎi 拽 ㄓㄨㄞˇ	zhuī 追 ㄓㄨㄟ	zhuān 專 ㄓㄨㄢ	zhǔn 準 ㄓㄨㄣˇ	zhuāng 裝 ㄓㄨㄤ	zhōng 中 ㄓㄨㄥ					**zh**
					chū 出 ㄔㄨ		chuō 戳 ㄔㄨㄛ	chuǎi 揣 ㄔㄨㄞˇ	chuī 吹 ㄔㄨㄟ	chuān 川 ㄔㄨㄢ	chūn 春 ㄔㄨㄣ	chuáng 床 ㄔㄨㄤˊ	chóng 蟲 ㄔㄨㄥˊ					**ch**
					shū 書 ㄕㄨ	shuā 刷 ㄕㄨㄚ	shuō 說 ㄕㄨㄛ	shuài 帥 ㄕㄨㄞˋ	shuǐ 水 ㄕㄨㄟˇ	shuān 拴 ㄕㄨㄢ	shùn 順 ㄕㄨㄣˋ	shuāng 雙 ㄕㄨㄤ						**sh**
					rú 如 ㄖㄨˊ		ruò 弱 ㄖㄨㄛˋ		ruì 瑞 ㄖㄨㄟˋ	ruǎn 軟 ㄖㄨㄢˇ	rùn 閏 ㄖㄨㄣˋ		róng 容 ㄖㄨㄥˊ					**r**
					zū 租 ㄗㄨ		zuó 昨 ㄗㄨㄛˊ		zuì 最 ㄗㄨㄟˋ	zuàn 賺 ㄗㄨㄢˋ	zūn 尊 ㄗㄨㄣ		zòng 粽 ㄗㄨㄥˋ					**z**
					cù 促 ㄘㄨˋ		cuò 錯 ㄘㄨㄛˋ		cuì 脆 ㄘㄨㄟˋ	cuàn 篡 ㄘㄨㄢˋ	cūn 村 ㄘㄨㄣ		cóng 從 ㄘㄨㄥˊ					**c**
					sū 蘇 ㄙㄨ		suǒ 所 ㄙㄨㄛˇ		suì 歲 ㄙㄨㄟˋ	suān 酸 ㄙㄨㄢ	sūn 孫 ㄙㄨㄣ		sòng 送 ㄙㄨㄥˋ					**s**

LEARN TO WRITE
by lesson

Lesson	Chinese		English
1	人	rén	people, person
	山	shān	mountain
	口	kǒu	mouth
2	你	nǐ	you
	好	hǎo	good
	我	wǒ	I, me
	是	shì	is, am, are
	他	tā	he, him
	們	men	[plural word]
3	一	yī	one
	二	èr	two
	三	sān	three
	四	sì	four
	五	wǔ	five
	六	liù	six
	七	qī	seven
	八	bā	eight
	九	jiǔ	nine
	十	shí	ten
4	誰	shéi	who
	她	tā	she, her
	老	lǎo	old
	師	shī	teacher
	幾	jǐ	how many
	歲	suì	year of age
	兩	liǎng	two
5	這	zhè	this
	那	nà	that
	什	shé	what
	麼	me	[word ending]
	嗎	ma	[question word]
	的	de	[possesive particle]
	不	bù	no, not
6	家	jiā	home
	有	yǒu	to have, there is/are
	個	ge	[measure word]
	爸	bà	father
	媽	mā	mother
	哥	gē	elder brother
	姊	jiě	elder sister
	弟	dì	younger brother
	妹	mèi	younger sister
7	寵	chǒng	to spoil
	物	wù	object, thing
	隻	zhī	[measure word]
	狗	gǒu	dog
	馬	mǎ	horse
	很	hěn	very
	大	dà	big
	小	xiǎo	little
	沒	méi	[negative word]
8	中	zhōng	center, middle
	國	guó	nation
	美	měi	beautiful
	加	jiā	to add, plus
	拿	ná	to take
	也	yě	also
	會	huì	to be able to, can
	説	shuō	to speak, to say
9	喜	xǐ	to like; happy
	歡	huān	happy
	運	yùn	to transport; luck
	動	dòng	to move
	打	dǎ	to hit, to play (tennis...etc.)
	球	qiú	ball
	去	qù	to go
	吧	ba	[suggestion word]
10	朋	péng	friend
	友	yǒu	friend
	叫	jiào	to be called, call
	上	shàng	to go to
	年	nián	year
	級	jí	grade, level
	和	hé, hàn	and
	同	tóng	same; together
	學	xué	to study, to learn
11	真	zhēn	really
	餓	è	hungry
	吃	chī	to eat
	想	xiǎng	to think
	渴	kě	thirsty
	喝	hē	to drink
	菜	cài	dish, vegetable
	飯	fàn	cooked rice, meal